The Socialist Economy

The Socialist Economy
Theory and practice

Tom Bottomore

⬛ HARVESTER
⬛ WHEATSHEAF

New York London Toronto Sydney Tokyo Singapore

First published 1990 by
Harvester Wheatsheaf
66 Wood Lane End, Hemel Hempstead
Hertfordshire HP2 4RG
A division of
Simon & Schuster International Group

Typeset in 10/12pt Times
by Witwell Ltd, Southport

Printed and bound in Great Britain by
Billing and Sons Limited, Worcester

British Library Cataloguing in Publication Data

Bottomore, Tom, *1920*-
    The socialist economy : theory and practice.
    1. Communist countries.   Economic policies
    I. Title
    330.91717

    ISBN 0-7450-0118-1
    ISBN 0-7450-0119-X pbk

---

1 2 3 4 5   94 93 92 91 90

Contents

Introduction: Socialist economy and socialist society

Socialism, as a political doctrine and a social movement, has never set itself purely economic aims. From the beginning its ideal was the creation of a new type of society, or, as Gramsci expressed it, 'a new civilization'. Some critics indeed have argued that socialist thinkers, at any rate until the 1920s, largely ignored the question of how a socialist economy would actually function; and Mises (1920, 1922), in one of the most extreme and vitriolic attacks, claimed to show that it would not function at all.

In this book I shall consider whether, and for what reasons, earlier socialist thinkers did unduly neglect the economic problems of socialism; what has been learned, or can still be learned, from the debates of the 1930s about socialist calculation and central planning; and finally, what new conceptions and practices have emerged from the experience of socialist development in the post-war period. My approach to these questions is sociological, setting economic relations in their wider social and cultural framework, and this corresponds broadly with the idea of the connections between economy and society that has generally been expressed in socialist thought.

There are, to be sure, diverse conceptions of socialism,[1] but what is common to almost all of them is a conviction of the fundamental importance of the economy in shaping social life as a whole; an idea which found its most trenchant expression in Marx's social theory. I shall interpret that theory, which has been reformulated, modified

1

and 'reconstructed' by many later thinkers,[2] not as asserting a universal and strict determination of the political and cultural 'superstructure' by the economic 'base', but as arguing that the manner in which human beings produce and reproduce the material conditions of their existence is a major factor in the creation of a whole 'form of life'; or, in Marx's own words, that the 'mode of production should not be regarded simply as the reproduction of the physical existence of individuals. It is far more a definite form of activity of these individuals, a definite way of expressing their life, a definite *mode of life*' (Marx and Engels, 1845–6, vol. I, section IA).

Marx goes on to say, in the same passage, that what individuals are 'coincides' with their production, 'with *what* they produce and *how* they produce'; and it is this conception which has largely guided socialist periodizations of history, up to the advent of modern capitalism and the movement towards socialism. The crucial feature is *how* human beings produce, which encompasses both the technical means of production (and notably since the nineteenth century the spectacular advance of science and technology, which also profoundly affects *what* is produced), and the way in which the social labour process is organized; that is to say, the social relations of production formed by the distinctive characteristics, in different historical periods, of the 'owners of the conditions of production' and the 'direct producers'. In modern capitalist society, according to Marx's analysis, the social relations of production, which establish the framework of a distinct mode of life, are constituted by the capitalist ownership of means of production and by wage labour; and the essence of the socialist alternative – not only in its Marxist versions – has always been the transformation of private ownership into social ownership, which Marx expressed by referring to a future society of 'associated producers'.

The 'associated mode of production', as Marx called it in the third volume of *Capital* (1894, ch. 23), or more generally 'cooperative production', was not treated in the socialist literature of the nineteenth century as having only an economic significance, but as a vital element in the constitution of a new form of society in which individuals would no longer be dependent upon dominant minorities, but would be able to develop freely in a social environment which they took a full and equal part in creating. At the same time, as natural beings, they would still be subject to material constraints, and Marx was more realistic than some other socialist thinkers or prophets in recognizing that

> the realm of freedom . . . [lies] . . . outside the sphere of material production proper. Just as the savage must wrestle with nature in order to satisfy his wants, to maintain and reproduce his life, so also must civilized man, and he must do it in all forms of society and under any possible mode of production. With his development the realm of natural necessity expands, because his wants increase; but at the same time the forces of production, by which these wants are satisfied, also increase. Freedom in this field cannot consist of anything else but the fact that socialized humanity, the associated producers, regulate their exchange with nature rationally, bring it under their common control, instead of being ruled by it as by some blind power, and accomplish their task with the least expenditure of energy and under such conditions as are proper and worthy for human beings. Nevertheless, this always remains a realm of necessity. (Marx, 1894, vol. III, ch. 48)

Hence Marx's further contention that a precondition of freedom is the reduction of working hours and that 'a nation is truly rich when, instead of working twelve hours, it works only six' (Marx, 1857-8, p. 706).

On the other hand, Marx certainly anticipated a continued growth of material wealth, and above all a virtually unlimited development of human powers of production, in socialist society; but this view raises difficult questions, which have increasingly preoccupied socialist thinkers, about the human relation to nature and the possibility or desirability of setting out deliberately to satisfy in the fullest measure all conceivable material needs, rather than encouraging the emergence of a new structure of needs in which non-material needs acquire greater importance.[3] True, there are in Marx's own writings occasional references to the ecological conditions of human existence, as in the passage in *Capital* (1894, vol. III, ch. 46) which he concludes by saying that 'Even a whole society, a nation, or all contemporary societies taken together, are not the absolute owners of the earth. They are only its occupants, its beneficiaries, and like a good paterfamilias have to leave it in improved condition to succeeding generations'; and his social philosophy as a whole – particularly in the early writings, though not only there – emphasizes human freedom and creativity outside the sphere of work, along with a steady reduction of the time devoted to that sphere, rather than the expansion of material production as such.

Nevertheless, in the actual development of socialist economies in the twentieth century, as well as in socialist thought more generally, there has undoubtedly been an intense preoccupation with sheer economic growth, and in the past decade or so with the new prospects for growth opened up by the 'scientific–technological revolution'. Many factors have contributed to this particular orientation of socialist thought and practice:

1. The advent of socialism in countries which were, for the most part, economically backward, agrarian and peasant societies, and the perceived need for extensive and rapid industrialization.
2. The extent of poverty in the capitalist societies during the depression of the 1930s and the commitment to eradicate it.[4]
3. The rapid post-war expansion of 'organized capitalism', characterized by large-scale state intervention, partial planning and very high rates of growth, and the need for socialist societies (as well as socialist governments when they come to power in capitalist countries) to compete effectively with capitalism in the provision of high material levels of living.
4. The conflict between power blocs which has led to the investment of immense resources in the development of ever more sophisticated and expensive weapons.

This addiction to growth has, of course, been contested by many thinkers in the socialist movement itself, and it has always been qualified by the commitment to broader social ideals. Within, or on the fringes of, Marxist thought the 'critical theorists' of the Frankfurt School[5] expressed with particular force their opposition to the main tendencies of development in advanced industrial society in all its forms, arguing that the drive to dominate nature through science and technology necessarily involves the domination of human beings and is the major obstacle to emancipation.[6] In the past few decades important ecology movements have emerged in the industrial countries, most prominently in West Germany where the Green Party has had significant electoral success. These movements have been supported by many socialists[7] and have themselves had an important influence on the ideas and policies of socialist parties, giving a new salience to aims which had become obscured by the concentration of attention on material production.

But in recognizing the development of new attitudes to economic growth we should not overlook the fact that socialist thought and practice always envisaged growth in the context of a more comprehensive reorganization of social life, and also largely assumed that the problem of scarcity – in the sense of an inability to satisfy the basic material needs of all members of society, at the level of civilization already attained – would already have been overcome by the development of capitalism itself. Hence, in examining the achievements and problems of the present-day socialist societies we have to consider not only what is produced, in what conditions it is produced, and the efficiency of the process of production as a whole, but also how the product of the social labour process is allocated and distributed. There are, of course, great differences between the socialist industrial countries and those socialist countries of the Third World which have only recently embarked on the process of economic development and industrialization; but what is evident in all these societies is the sustained commitment, from the outset, to the widest possible extension of public services – education, health care and other welfare services, the provision of housing, public transport and recreational facilities – within the limits of their economic resources; and in this respect they have achieved some notable successes. George and Manning (1980) note that 'social policy is more ambitious in its aims in the Soviet Union than in welfare capitalist societies', even though 'not always more comprehensive in its achievements' (which will be affected by the rate of economic growth), and that, 'the dominant ideology of the Soviet Union provides a more secure environment for the growth of social policy' (pp. 168-9).[8] In the developing countries the most striking successes (for example, in Cuba and more recently in Nicaragua) have been in overcoming illiteracy and providing basic health care for the mass of the population; the major problems those of meeting the rapidly rising expectations of their populations while at the same time investing heavily in the infrastructure of production, countering the tendencies towards the growth of bureaucracy and a new centralization of power, and coping with the hostility of the capitalist world, which is expressed in economic pressure and sometimes direct intervention (particularly by the

United States).[9]

The economy, therefore, has a crucial importance in the creation of a socialist society in two respects. First, the social ownership of the principal means of production is intended to eliminate the domination of society by a particular class, and to establish the conditions in which all members of society can participate actively in the management and development of their productive resources, including the use of their own labour power. But this goal of widespread participation has encountered many obstacles in the actual development of socialist societies, and in the past few decades numerous projects and experiments designed to increase participation by a thoroughgoing reform of the economic system have taken shape. These changes, the controversies which surround them, the new directions of socialist thought with regard to central planning, self-management and markets, are major subjects for analysis in the following chapters.

Second, an efficient, well-managed, productive economy is an indispensable condition for attaining the broader aims of socialism – the elimination of poverty, increase of leisure time, extensive social services, a high level of education and general culture. But in this respect, too, the existing socialist societies have faced serious difficulties, and ever since the 1920s there has been much debate about the efficiency of centrally planned economies. This question, which will be examined in Chapter 3 below, raises some larger issues, broadly of two kinds. In the first place, the problem of efficiency may be directly linked with that of participation, and the alleged deficiencies of central planning, as we shall see, may be explained in part by the stifling of initiative, responsibility, choice and decision, among individuals and groups in society at large. But second, we have to consider the notion of efficiency itself in a wider context. A socialist economy serves a socialist society, and the rationalization of production in order to achieve an ever increasing flow of material goods should not be given an absolute priority regardless of such considerations as working conditions and hours of work, the environment and the depletion of natural resources, or whether what is produced adds appreciably to the quality of life and the level of civilization. These are, however, very complex issues and I shall examine them more closely in later chapters.

What will be evident, I hope, throughout this book, but should be emphasized very strongly at the outset, is that I do not claim to possess any incontrovertible criterion of what socialism *really is*, but simply a general conception of a socialist society (which certainly excludes some other types of society) within which a considerable variety of economic and social arrangements is possible. Socialism, like every human activity or form of life, is a historical phenomenon and no one can reasonably pretend to foresee in detail how it will evolve, or precisely how future generations will resolve, or perhaps sometimes fail to resolve, the problems that its further development generates. In this spirit I am inclined to take as a kind of motto for the present work the observation that Engels made *à propos* of another matter. Replying to a letter from Kautsky about the problem of excessive population growth (an issue often raised by opponents of socialism in the nineteenth century, on Malthusian grounds), Engels (1 February 1881) wrote:

> Of course the abstract possibility exists that the number of human beings will become so great that limits will have to be set to its increase. But if at some point communist society should find itself obliged to regulate the production of human beings, as it has already regulated the production of things, it will be precisely and only this society which carries it out without difficulty. . . . In any case, it is a matter for those people [in communist society] to decide if, when and how they act, and what means they wish to employ, and I do not feel called upon to offer them suggestions or advice. I daresay they will be quite as clever as we are.

Notes

1. Schumpeter (1942, pp. 170–1) claimed that socialism is so 'culturally indeterminate' that it cannot be precisely defined except in purely economic terms, but this is a considerable exaggeration, as I shall argue later.
2. See, in particular, Habermas (1976) and Larrain (1986).
3. There is an excellent discussion of this question, in relation to Marx's own thought, in Heller (1976), and a comprehensive general discussion in Springborg (1981).
4. Postan (1967) observed that an 'ideology of growth' emerged in part from earlier preoccupations with full employment which had their source in the controversies of the 1930s: 'Full employment eventually

developed into a policy and an economic philosophy much wider in its implications . . . into a policy of economic growth.'
5. For a general account of the school see Bottomore (1984b).
6. See especially Marcuse (1964), and for a more general discussion Leiss (1972). I consider many of these arguments exaggerated and misguided and I have criticized them in Bottomore (1984b).
7. See the discussion in Bahro (1982), especially the essay on 'Ecology crisis and socialist ideas', which also considers the relation of Marx's thought to ecology, observing that 'Marx already perceived the contradiction between capitalist production and nature. It was just that this was not yet so acute for him to place it at the centre of his analysis' (p. 30).
8. See also the excellent account of social policy in Hungary by Ferge (1979).
9. For a more detailed account see White (1983).

1

The nineteenth-century vision

The ideas of 'socialism' and 'communism',[1] and socialist movements, spread rapidly in Europe from the 1830s. Both the ideas and
the movements had important antecedents in the social criticism
and revolts of earlier times, but what was distinctive in the
nineteenth century was the extent of the movements, their organization on a national and even international scale, their growing
identification with the specific situation and interests of the industrial working class, and at the same time the systematic elaboration
of a new 'world view'. The latter was first signalled by the
appearance of the word 'socialism' itself, and it then developed in a
great variety of forms: in socialist doctrines from the Saint-
Simonians to the Marxists; in social experiments, and the literature
about them, inspired by Robert Owen, the Fourierists and many
others; in major political movements during the revolutions of 1848
and in the Paris Commune; and in social movements which created
trade unions, cooperative societies and a host of educational and
cultural institutions.

Marx and Engels, in the *Communist Manifesto* (1848), were
highly critical of the early 'utopian socialists', observing that
because 'the economic situation . . . does not as yet offer to them
the material conditions for the emancipation of the proletariat',
they have to search for 'new social laws' to bring those conditions
about, and paint 'fantastic pictures of future society'. In Marxist
thought, and in much other socialist thought, which inspired the

formation and development of new political parties in the latter part of the nineteenth century, attention was concentrated upon the economic development of capitalism and the organization of the industrial working class as an effective political force. But the Utopian element did not disappear from the socialist movement, and indeed it revived strongly towards the end of the century in two widely read and influential novels, Edward Bellamy's *Looking Backward* (1887) and William Morris's *News from Nowhere* (1890). Both novels expounded a vision of a new society from which injustice, poverty and crime would be eliminated, and in which a complete equality would prevail. In both cases the effective functioning of the new social system depended ultimately upon a radical transformation of human nature, so that the sentiments favourable to peaceful cooperation, social responsibility and non-acquisitiveness became predominant. Morris had little to say in his novel about the economic organization of his Utopia, but Bellamy, on the other hand, devoted much attention to economic questions and conceived the economic structure of the new society as the outcome of the trust movement in American industry: 'the epoch of the trusts had ended in the Great Trust' (1887, p. 41). Industry would be centrally directed by the government and production would be carried on by an 'industrial army' in which everyone between the ages of twenty-one and forty-five would serve.

Bellamy emphasized liberty as well as equality, particularly in the sphere of consumption, where every citizen would be free to spend the annual credit assigned to him as his share of the national product in any way he pleased, and production would respond to consumer preferences. But the 'industrial army' was to be very autocratically constituted, as was the national government, and Bellamy largely ignored the dangers to both freedom and equality inherent in this extreme centralization and the emergence of a powerful bureaucracy. The success of the new society that he portrayed depended essentially, as I have suggested, on a change in the orientation of human purposes from self-seeking and competitiveness to cooperation and a subordination of individual reward to the general welfare; and this is still more apparent in *News from Nowhere* where Morris, who was repelled by Bellamy's picture of a completely planned social order, depicts the future society as one that is based upon voluntary, spontaneous cooperation without any elaborate organization of the economy, government or administration. In any case, as Morris explicitly said, his Utopia was 'not a prediction, but a description of the kind of society in which he would feel most at home', his 'personal vision of the good society' (Cole 1954, p. 423). As such it evidently appealed to many people at the end of the nineteenth century, and it still has its appeal in the vastly changed circumstances of today.

Although Marx rejected Utopian socialism as having been largely superseded by the development of the working-class movement, there were undoubtedly Utopian elements, as well as many unresolved problems, in his own brief and scattered comments on the future 'society of associated producers'. As Heller (1976, pp. 118–30) has noted, in his conception of this form of society 'Marx is working with an entirely new structure of needs' in which human labour will (a) cease to be 'alienated' (i.e. performed under external compulsion), and (b) become *travail attractif* (i.e. 'a field for the self-realization of the human personality' and hence a vital need). But these two aspects are not treated by Marx in precisely the same way in different writings. In the *Grundrisse* both conditions are met: labour ceases to be alienated and it also becomes *travail attractif* (as intellectual labour). In *Capital*, vol. III, however, Marx declares that labour and material production always remain a 'realm of necessity', and the realm of freedom only begins where labour ceases; all that can be achieved in the sphere of material production is a humane organization of the labour process as a cooperative activity and the direction of production to the satisfaction of 'true social needs'. But as Heller pertinently asks: how can 'true social needs' be measured; how can the diversity of individual needs and their rapid changes be provided for; who makes the decisions about how productive capacity should be allocated? On the last point, Marx would no doubt have replied: *everyone* (i.e. all the associated producers). Yet the difficulties are evident and, as Heller comments; 'How can every individual make such decisions? Marx did not answer this question, because for him it did not arise. For us, however, in our times, it has become perhaps the most decisive question of all'.

It is a question (to be explored more fully in later chapters) which has now to be considered not only in theoretical or speculative terms, but in the light of the historical experience we have gained from the movements towards socialism in modern capitalist societies and from the diverse attempts to construct socialist societies. This is not to say that the Utopian elements in socialism ought now to be discarded, or have in effect been discarded, in favour of some kind of 'new realism', although that may well accord with the dispirited political mood of this *fin de siècle*. Heller's study concludes optimistically that the Utopian aspects of Marx's ideas on the future society of associated producers remain *fertile*, providing a norm 'against which we can measure the reality and value of our ideas' and embodying 'the most beautiful aspiration of mature humanity'; and in some of the social movements of the 1960s, which were surely not its ultimate manifestation, this aspiration found for a time a fresh and invigorating expression.[2]

In the nineteenth century, at all events, the various currents of Utopian socialist thought played an important part in the creation and development of new types of social organization: the early forms of trade unionism; the cooperative factories – described by Marx (*Capital*, vol. III, ch. 27) as a new mode of production 'within the old form' – and the broader consumer cooperative movement; and Friendly Societies as a major form of mutual aid. At the same time socialist ideas began to be more widely and systematically diffused through the development of mass political parties. Some of these parties were Marxist; notably those in Germany and Austria, which were growing rapidly by the end of the century and had created for millions of workers a distinctive way of life that has been described as taking on the character of 'a state within a state' (Nettl 1965). Others were created either as the political arm of the trade union movement, concentrating on piecemeal legislative changes to improve the conditions of workers – as was largely the case with the British Labour Party – or more generally as parties which conceived the attainment of socialism as the outcome of a gradual process of economic and social reconstruction rather than a sudden revolutionary transformation.

The growth of mass parties, with their leaders, officials, newspapers, and numerous subsidiary or related organizations, and their continuous involvement in day-to-day politics, brought about changes in the formulation of socialist aims. While Utopian ideas continued to provide a general stimulus to the socialist movement, the political parties had necessarily to engage in struggles for the achievement of interim reforms which would improve the conditions of the working class – universal suffrage, trade union rights, factory legislation, the expansion of education and of health and welfare services. By the end of the century the outcome of these reforming activities came to be seen by some socialists as an important element in the changes in capitalist society which required a more 'gradualist' conception of the transition to socialism.

One of the most influential formulations of this view appeared in a series of articles on 'problems of socialism' by Bernstein (1896–8), subsequently expounded more comprehensively in a book (1899) which set off the 'revisionist debate' among Marxist socialists. Bernstein's arguments were directed primarily against an 'economic collapse' theory of the demise of capitalism and the advent of socialism, and against the conception of an increasing polarization of classes, accompanied by intensifying class conflict, in capitalist society. His ideas are conveniently summarized in a note found among his papers: 'Peasants do not sink; middle class does not disappear; crises do not grow ever larger; misery and serfdom do not increase. There *is* increase in insecurity, dependence, social distance, social character of production, functional superfluity of property owners' (Gay 1952, p. 244). In the last chapter of his book Bernstein discussed 'the tasks and possibilities of social democracy' in the light of his revision of Marxist theory, and dealt with three main issues. First, he drew attention to the importance of cooperative organizations as 'the easiest accessible form of association for the working class' (p. 125) which 'bear in themselves enough of the element of socialism to develop into worthy and indispensable levers for the socialist emancipation' (p. 187), though he was critical of those conceptions – Utopian in his view – which regarded producer cooperatives as the principal way of organizing socialist production (pp. 109–20). Second, Bernstein emphasized the role of democratic institutions and the activities of numerous independent self-governing associations in the movement towards socialism: 'the conquest of the democracy, the formation of political and social organs of the democracy, is the indispensable preliminary condition to the realisation of socialism' (p. 163). Third, he noted the significance of municipal socialism in the advance towards a socialist society and as a field of fruitful activity alongside the parliamentary struggle.

Bernstein had been greatly influenced by the ideas of the Fabian socialists (with whom he established close relations during his exile in England from 1888 to 1901) which were another major factor in the revision of socialist conceptions at the end of the nineteenth century; indeed Bernard Shaw, in his preface to the 1908 reprint of the *Fabian Essays*, claimed that: 'Since 1889 the Socialist movement has been competely transformed throughout Europe; and the result of this transformation may fairly be described as Fabian Socialism' (1931, p. xxxiii). The main tenets of the new conception were set out in a historical essay by Sidney Webb. In the first place it was evolutionist (explicitly related to the theories of Comte, Darwin and Spencer), and in consequence 'gradualist': 'No philosopher now looks for anything but the gradual evolution of the new order from the old, without break of continuity or abrupt change of the entire social tissue at any point during the process' (1931, p. 29). The Fabian thinkers, therefore, were totally opposed to all Utopian or 'catastrophic' views of the transition to socialism: 'history shews us no example of the sudden substitution of Utopian and revolutionary romance' (*ibid.*). Webb then continued by associating the socialist movement with democracy: 'The main stream which has borne European society towards Socialism during the past 100 years is the irresistible progress of Democracy' (p. 31); and he summarized his view by saying that socialists now realize that 'important organic changes can only be . . . democratic, and thus acceptable to a majority of the people, and prepared for in the minds of all . . . gradual, and thus causing no dislocation, however rapid may be the rate of progress', and in Britain at any rate, 'constitutional and peaceful', (p. 32). Webb also laid stress upon municipal socialism (and Bernstein followed him in this respect), observing that 'it is the municipalities which have done most to "socialize" our industrial life' (p. 47).

But the growth of socialist parties brought another change beyond the increasing involvement in reformist politics and the adoption of a more gradualist outlook. The eventual socialist economy came to be conceived more explicitly in terms of the nationalization of major industries and the introduction of centralized economic planning, while the ideas of cooperative production and self-management by the 'associated producers' were largely dismissed as Utopian fantasies.[3] Thus Annie Besant, in her contribution to the *Fabian Essays* on industry under socialism, though she allowed for some urban and regional organization of industry, argued that concurrently with this would proceed 'the taking over of the great centralised industries, centralised for us by capitalists, who thus unconsciously pave the way for their own supersession' (Shaw, 1931, p. 146). The argument is close to that of Marx and later Marxists concerning the process of 'socialization of the economy' reaching fulfilment in a socialist society where, as Hilferding (1910, p. 27) later expressed it, production would be regulated by 'the local, regional or national commissars' who would 'shape, with conscious foresight, the whole economic life of the communities of which they are the appointed representatives and leaders, in accordance with the needs of the members', and the labour process as well as the distribution of products would be 'subject to central control'.

By the beginning of the twentieth century the socialist parties, whether they were Marxist or not, had reached very similar conclusions about how a socialist economy should be organized through the nationalization of major industries and centralized economic planning. But there was little experience of operating publicly owned industries, outside the limited field of muni-cipal enterprise, and the projects for socialist reconstruction were couched in very general and abstract terms, without much consider-ation in detail of the problems that might emerge. It was recognized, to be sure, that the future society could not be completely planned in advance (and for that reason the Utopian schemes were rejected); Annie Besant (Shaw 1931, pp. 140–1) aimed 'to forecast, not the far-off future, but the next social stage . . . to work out changes practicable among men and women as we know them', while Karl Kautsky (1902, p. 105) in his essay on 'the day after the revolution', expressed very clearly the view that after the conquest of political power 'problems will arise of which we know nothing and many with which we are occupied today will by that time be solved. New means to the solutions of these different problems will also arise of which we today have no suspicion.'

Kautsky went on, however, to examine more closely than was usual among socialist thinkers some of the immediate problems that might be encountered in constructing a socialist economy. One of these was the incentive to work, which he thought would depend partly on working-class discipline, though this would be a 'democratic discipline' presupposing a 'democratic organization of labour' and a 'democratic factory' (p. 126); and he also noted that there would be various forms of social property – national, municipal and cooperative – while private property could still exist in many means of production (p. 127). But the effects of this working-class discipline would also need to be complemented by making work itself more attractive, reducing the hours of labour and improving conditions in the workplace (p. 128). These were ideas that had already been briefly formulated by Marx, though as the discussion by Heller, cited earlier, indicates, the problems are more complex than was foreseen by socialists in the nineteenth century.

Kautsky also expounded very clearly the role of money in a socialist economy:

> Money is the simplest means known up to the present time which makes it possible in as complicated a mechanism as that of the modern productive process, with its tremendous far-reaching division of labour, to secure the circulation of products and their distribution to the individual members of society. It is the means which makes it possible for each one to satisfy his necessities according to his individual inclination (to be sure within the bounds of his economic power). As a means to such circulation money will be found indispensable until something better is discovered. To be sure many of its functions, especially that of the measure of value, will disappear, at least in internal commerce. (p. 129)

He then went on to discuss how the incomes of workers might be increased under socialism, pointing out that because of the need for investment and public expenditure there would be 'none too much remaining over from the present income of the capitalist to be applied to the raising of wages' (p. 136), and emphasizing as the main factor a rapid expansion of production. This, he argued, could be achieved mainly by a rationalization of production which would concentrate it in larger, more efficient plants, and by the elimination of economic crises. But Kautsky, unlike Marx in the *Grundrisse*, did not specifically include the progress of science and technology among the important factors affecting the productivity of labour, and he did not therefore discuss the question of how technological innovation would be organized in a socialist society, or whether it might be impeded by the development of a bureaucratic system of state management. In the last part of his essay, however, Kautsky did suggest some variations and limits in the socialization of production. He made clear, first, that there would be municipal and cooperative enterprises alongside the large state-owned concerns; and second, that not all production would be socialized, and many individual producers would remain active:

> . . . the greatest diversity and possibility of change will rule . . . The most manifold forms of property in the means of production – national, municipal, cooperatives of consumption and production, and private – can exist beside each other in a socialist society, the most diverse forms of industrial organization . . . of remuneration of labour . . . of circulation of products. . . . The same manifold character of economic mechanism that exists today is possible in a socialist society. (p. 166)

Apart from agriculture, where Kautsky stressed the important role of small farmers, a major sphere for the development of small-scale and individual enterprises was, in his view, that of 'intellectual production'. The educational system and scientific research would need to be nationally organized, but in the arts and literature free individual activity must prevail, and Kautsky summed up his ideas in the phrase 'Communism in material production, anarchism in the intellectual' (p. 183).

Although socialist thinkers, as I have illustrated, became increasingly preoccupied with the question of organizing and managing an economy based upon the socialization of large-scale enterprises, and relying to a great extent upon central planning, Utopian ideas did not vanish completely from the socialist movement. The Utopian novels of Bellamy and Morris were themselves published late in the nineteenth century and were very widely read. In particular, the idea of self-management by the 'associated producers' remained potent and assumed new forms; for example, in the French syndicalist movement, which also strongly influenced the workers' movement in Italy and Spain, in the American Industrial Workers of the World, and in the guild socialist movement in Britain. The latter developed in a climate of opinion that owed much to Morris, and 'News from Nowhere . . . might be taken as the vision that the guild socialists strove to interpret in a form appropriate to the twentieth century' (Glass 1966, p. 8).[4]

Somewhat later, towards the end of the First World War, the idea of self-management received a new impulse from the emergence of workers' and soldiers' councils and the development of what came to be called the 'council movement'. Karl Renner (1921) analysed this phenomenon in terms of an opposition between a 'purely political democracy' and 'economic democracy', characterizing the 'council system' as one in which political functions or political significance are assigned 'to collectivities which are formed by the common interests of an occupation, a status group, or a class'; and besides citing the example of the Russian 'dictatorship of workers', peasants' and soldiers' councils' (which he did not examine further) he discussed the work of the Webbs on industrial democracy, and the ideas of Guild Socialism in Britain. Renner recognized the importance of what he called 'voluntary economic democracies' (such as the trades unions, cooperatives and Friendly Societies), but he concluded that the role of the state and political democracy were crucial and paramount in regulating conflicts of interest between various sectional groups in society, and he did not directly address the issue of workers' self-management, which was nevertheless very prominent in those sections of the council movement that focused attention on the 'factory councils' as a means of achieving industrial democracy (Bauer 1923, Bricianer 1978, Gramsci 1919–20, Pribićević 1959).

The idea of self-management as an essential feature of socialist society has remained vigorously alive up to the present time. It found practical expression in the Yugoslav system of workers' self-management (Broekmeyer 1970) which has had an increasing influence, during the past two decades, on the economic reforms in other socialist countries from Eastern Europe to China; and in a more Utopian and speculative form it played an important part in the radical social movements of the 1960s, expressed in the concept of 'participatory democracy' (Jacobs and Landau 1966). One reason for its continued, and even growing, influence in socialist thought is undoubtedly the increasing dissatisfaction with some of the consequences of bureaucratic administration of state-owned enterprises in capitalist countries, and still more with the authoritarian and cumbersome management of the whole economy in socialist countries; a dissatisfaction which concerns both the human relations within the enterprise or industrial sector, and, in varying degrees, but most obviously in some socialist countries, the overall efficiency of the system of production and distribution.

But an economy based upon self-management of individual enterprises itself encounters problems which have been widely debated, in response to the criticisms that were levelled at the ideas expounded by the council movement, the syndicalists and the Guild Socialists,[5] and in the light of experience of the actual functioning of cooperative production and self-management. Two issues have been crucially important in this debate – the extent to which effective participation in management can really be achieved in enterprises which differ greatly in size, complexity and technological sophistication; and the ways in which individual enterprises should be related to the national and international economy, through central or regional planning or through market mechanisms (more or less strictly regulated) – and they will be considered in detail in later chapters.

By the early years of the twentieth century the socialist vision had assumed, as I have illustrated, a diversity of forms, and in the course of this century it has become ever more diverse, in theory and in practice. But this growing diversity, marked especially by the rift between the authoritarian or totalitarian socialism of Eastern Europe and the democratic socialism of Western Europe, was accompanied after 1945 by a steady advance of the 'socialist idea' in many of the capitalist countries, and by a gradual extension of broadly socialist policies and institutions. In most of the West European countries membership of socialist parties, and the socialist vote, increased substantially (though Britain was a notable exception), and in many countries socialist governments have been in office for longer or shorter periods (Bottomore 1984a, ch. 11). Since the mid-1970s, however, there has been a notable resurgence of capitalism, and the virtues of private enterprise and a market economy have been widely and vigorously extolled (again with exceptional fervour and effect in Britain, reflecting the weakness of the socialist movement). This change has reawakened discussion of the content and prospects of the 'socialist idea' in terms often reminiscent of the revisionist debate provoked by Bernstein at the end of the nineteenth century,[6] and the debate has been given fresh impetus by the reforms that are now under way in the USSR and other socialist countries.

An important part of the debate concerns the political institutions of a socialist society, and above all the question of democracy, pluralism and individual liberty; but the economic structure of socialism, which is linked in many respects with the political problems, remains a crucial issue, and is the principal subject of this book. In assessing the current rethinking and restructuring of socialism we do not need to adopt either of two extreme positions: one which clings obdurately to past formulae and to the idea of a sudden miraculous transformation of human nature and society on 'the day after the revolution'; or one which rejects almost the entire past along with any Utopian vision, in favour of accommodation to what seems immediately, or in the short term, feasible. Nor do we need to fear, or to regard as symptoms of a profound and perhaps terminal crisis, the critical reassessments and reforms which are now taking place. Socialism, like capitalism, is a historical phenomenon, subject to all kinds of change and processes of development or decay, and every generation has to face new situations, problems and opportunities – in large part inherited, to be sure, from the past – with which it must grapple as intelligently and resolutely as it can. No one can predict with any accuracy exactly what kind of world human beings will inhabit a hundred years from now, if they still have a world to inhabit; but we can at least be confident, I think, that the nineteenth-century vision of socialism has become an enduring part of the furniture of the human mind, and that the socialist idea and socialist practice, however greatly modified by new experience, will remain powerfully effective for a long time to come.

Notes

1. The terms 'socialism' and 'communism' were used more or less interchangeably in the early nineteenth century, although the former was more widely employed, and this practice continued through much of the century. Marx and Engels followed this usage to some extent and did not take strong exception even to the term 'social democratic' which had been adopted by some socialist parties, although Engels later (1894) expressed reservations, saying that while 'the word will pass muster' it was really unsuitable 'for a party whose economic programme is not merely socialist in general but specifically communist, and whose ultimate political aim is to overcome the entire state and consequently democracy as well.' Only in the twentieth century, particularly after the creation of the Third (Communist) International and of separate Communist parties, did the term 'communism' acquire a more distinctive meaning, embodying the idea of revolutionary action in con-

trast with socialism as a more peaceful, gradual and 'reformist' approach to social change, while at the same time communist society came to be represented (notably by Lenin) as a second, higher stage in the development of post-capitalist societies. On the diverse and changing usages see the article by Jászi (1934), Stanley Moore (1980), and the entries on 'Communism' and 'Socialism' in Bottomore (1983). In this book the term 'socialism' will be used to refer to all those movements which aim or have aimed to create a 'classless society' or, in one form or another, a 'society of associated producers', and to the diverse types of society which claim to have achieved, in some degree, those aims; and any necessary distinctions between different movements and societies will be made at the appropriate place in the text.

2. Another defence of Utopian thought was made by Otto Neurath (1919) who argued that 'we find in utopias prophetic trains of thought which remain closed to those who, proud of their sense of reality, stuck fast to yesterday and could not even control the present'; and he suggested that Utopias might be regarded as 'constructions of social engineers'. More generally, in his writing on economic planning (which will be discussed in the next chapter), he advocated the elaboration of 'alternative scientific utopias' as part of the planning process. See also the discussion in Landauer (1959, ch. 46).

3. For an illuminating discussion of 'statist', 'collectivist' and 'associationist' versions of socialism, see Yeo (1987).

4. Glass's study provides a good account of the background and development of Guild Socialism, in which G. D. H. Cole played a major role from 1913 to 1923 (see Cole 1920). Morris sketched his own vision of the future organization of industrial production in his essay 'A factory as it might be' (1907); and in the early 1950s I had the pleasure of visiting a workers' cooperative ('Boimondau'), engaged in the manufacture of watch cases in Valence in France, which had conjured this vision into reality.

5. See the comments by Renner (1921) and Glass (1966, ch. 7).

6. For an early reassessment, which raises many issues that are highly relevant to the present controversies see Kolakowski and Hampshire (1974).

2

Marxist conceptions of a socialist economy

Marx referred only in the most general terms, and on rare occasions, to the socialist mode of production, as that of the 'associated producers', or as the 'self-government of the producers', and in the *Grundrisse* (pp. 704–6) as an economy, such as had already begun to develop under capitalism, in which the 'creation of real wealth . . . depends upon the general state of science and the progress of technology' and 'general social knowledge has become a *direct productive force*'. For the most part, later Marxist thinkers, at the end of the nineteenth century and in the first decade of the twentieth century, continued to describe the socialist economy mainly in terms of a progression into public ownership of the large-scale enterprises and financial institutions which had become increasingly dominant in the capitalist economy, without considering in any detail how these public corporations would be managed or precisely how a centrally planned economy would function. As Landauer (1959, p. 1611) observed:

> In the last years before the First World War the groundwork was laid for the great advance of socialist theory in the interwar years, but this preparatory work was done in the main by some of the critics of socialism and not by the socialists themselves. The period from 1900 to 1914 was unfavourable to the emergence of a realistic theory of socialism because one wing of the socialist movement was committed to Marxism which offered no basis for such a theory, and the other wing was too much under the

influence of the historical and institutionalist schools . . . to be greatly interested in any sort of theoretical analysis.

The work of Karl Kautsky, as I indicated in the previous chapter, was rather exceptional in discussing (while rejecting, in Marx's terms, any intention of writing recipes for the kitchens of the future) some of the problems that would face a socialist regime after the social revolution, and in outlining an economic structure in which large state-owned enterprises would be complemented by cooperative production and by small-scale or individual private enterprise. Gradually, however, in the new conditions resulting from the growth of large working-class parties, which needed to present more detailed economic and social policies in their programmes, and especially after the Russian Revolution, which made the construction of a socialist economy an urgent practical question, Marxist thinkers were obliged to consider more carefully and thoroughly the nature of economic institutions and mechanisms in a socialist society.

In this reorientation of thought the experience of the 'war economy' during the First World War played an important part, and was analysed in various ways. Karl Renner (1916), in a series of articles on 'problems of Marxism', argued that the war economy had accelerated a process of 'the penetration of the private economy down to its elementary cells by the state' and the emergence of 'control of the whole private sector of the economy by willed and conscious regulation and direction', concluding that society had 'entered an era of state economy . . . though entirely within the framework of the capitalist economic order'. The socialization of the economy had taken an unforeseen course, in which, for the time being, the principal agents were 'all-powerful national states', and this posed new problems for the socialist movement. One important aspect of his argument, which he and other Austro-Marxists developed in later writings, was that a working-class government could build upon and extend the economic functions of the state that had already emerged in capitalist society and would not need to reconstruct the entire state machinery. At the same time there is apparent in Renner's discussion a concern about the 'all-powerful state'; this concern was later expressed much more strongly by Hilferding (1941), after the experience of the Stalinist regime in the Soviet Union and the National Socialist regime in Germany, in his thoroughgoing revision of the Marxist theory of the state.

Quite a different aspect of the war economy was given prominence by Otto Neurath in articles published between 1916 and 1920, more particularly after his experience as the creator and president of a central planning office in Bavaria in 1919. He described this experience in a lecture given to the Sociological Society of Vienna (1920), and began by observing that:

> At the beginning of the revolution people were as unprepared for the task of a socialist economy in Germany as they had been for a war economy when war broke out in 1914. . . . The German Social Democratic Party had not worked out an economic programme and was unable to put forward clearcut demands for socialization. . . . The technique of a socialist economy had been badly neglected. Instead, only criticism of the capitalist society was offered. . . . That was why, when revolution broke out, a commission for socialization had to be called to discuss the basic principles. Longwinded, sterile debates took place, showing disagreements of all sorts, without producing a uniform programme.

Neurath went on to describe briefly his work during the period of the short-lived Bavarian Soviet, and to make clear his own commitment to 'full socialization' and central planning as against the partial measures that were being introduced in Germany as a whole. His conception of a socialized economy was outlined in articles on the war economy and on the immediate post-war attempts at socialization which were collected in a volume entitled *Through the War Economy to the Natural Economy* (1919). In one of these articles (1917) he argued that the decline of the free trade economy was accompanied by the advance of an 'administrative economy' orientated towards an economy in kind, which 'seems to incline towards the furthering of a certain uniform shaping of the economic organization, based on centralized measures'. In a later report (1919) delivered to the Munich Workers' Council, he set out more fully his idea of a socialist economy:

> The total organization whose creation we discussed can raise the economic efficiency of the order of life only if it possesses an adequate economic plan. It is not enough to know the possibilities of production and consumption as a whole, one must be able to

follow the movement and fate of all raw materials and energies, of men and machines throughout the economy [and for this purpose] we need universal statistics which, in coordinated surveys, comprise whole countries or even the world . . . Economic plans would have to be designed by a special office which would look on the total national economy as a single giant concern. Money prices would not be important for its surveys, since within the framework of a planned economy such prices, as long as they continue at all, are fixed in an essentially arbitrary manner by associations, by the state or by other authorities, whereas previously they were automatic results of competition. The central office for measurement in kind, as we might call the office mentioned above, would have as one of its tasks the presentation of the economic process at any given time, but above all would have to design the economic plans for the future. . . . We must at long last free ourselves from outmoded prejudices and regard a large-scale economy in kind as a fully valid form of economy which is the more important today in that any completely planned economy amounts to an economy in kind. To socialize therefore means to further an economy in kind. . . . In a large-scale economy in kind, in a socialized economy, money no longer is a driving force. No longer is there a 'net profit' for which production occurs. Money could remain at best as a token for a claim on all sorts of goods and services which the individual consumer is given to enable him to arrange his consumption.

Neurath went on to consider some specific problems of a socialized economy: in particular, 'economic efficiency' – which he saw as being decided by direct comparisons and judgements (made by the economic central office and the people's representatives) of the desirability of alternative projects and plans – and what he called 'substitute incentives', largely in terms of bonuses for higher output, which involved a trend towards 'technicism'. His writings, up to the early 1920s, were the most forceful expression of the idea of a socialist economy as a 'moneyless' economy, which had, according to Landauer (1959, p. 1636) 'the value of a bold intellectual experiment which . . . calls into consciousness the reasons for valid opinions', and also provoked 'the appearance of the new, aggressive school of anti-socialists', led by Ludwig von Mises, though its ideas were consonant 'with suggestions made by Max Weber' (p. 1637). Mises insisted on the need for an accounting system based upon value units in any complex society, and his critical assault on socialist planning was the principal source of the 'calculation debate' of the 1920s and 1930s, which will be considered in Chapter 4 below.

At this point, however, it is worth noting that Neurath's conception of 'calculation in kind' is significant also from another aspect, since in principle it enables economic planning to take into account the use, as between generations, of non-renewable natural resources (raw materials and energy). Neurath himself, in a later essay (1928), raised this question in discussing the formulation of production plans for providing housing:

> One may choose between plans: those that with the same effort consume more raw materials than others are of course eliminated. More difficult is the case where higher consumption of raw materials goes with less work. The question might arise, should one protect coal mines or put greater strain on men? The answer depends for example on whether one thinks that hydraulic power may be sufficiently developed or that solar heat might come to be better used, etc. If one believes the latter, one may 'spend' coal more freely and will hardly waste human effort where coal can be used. If however one is afraid that when one generation uses too much coal thousands will freeze to death in the future, one might well use more human power and save coal. Such and many other non-technical matters determine the choice of a technically calculable plan. (p. 263)

Neurath, however, did not pursue the ecological issues and in general there was little interest, and very little debate, among Marxists concerning ecology (Martinez-Alier 1987, ch. 14). It is, however, an important subject for modern socialist thought and I shall return to it in a later chapter.

After the Russian Revolution the principal Marxist discussions of economic planning took place in, or with reference to, the Soviet Union. The Soviet planning experience, in its particular historical context, will be examined in the next chapter. Here, I shall confine myself to the discussions among Marxists in the period from the First World War to the 1930s, which also related to the attempts at partial planning in some West European countries and the consequences of the war economy. As I noted earlier, Renner (1916), in his articles on 'problems of Marxism', had drawn attention to the great expansion of state intervention in the economy and raised

questions about how the activities of the interventionist state could
be transformed in a socialist direction; and later, Hilferding (1927)
argued that post-war capitalism had moved towards an 'organized
economy' in which the 'capitalist principle of free competition' was
replaced by 'the socialist principle of planned production', and that
the present generation faced 'the problem of transforming – with
the help of the state, which consciously regulates society – an
economy organized and directed by the *capitalists* into one which is
directed by the *democratic state*'. The Austro-Marxists clearly
conceived the socialist economy as one in which production would
be dominated by large state enterprises, with public ownership of
the financial institutions as a major element, and directed by a
central plan, and this was also, as we have seen, the view of
Neurath, who was broadly in sympathy with them and contributed
regularly to their journal *Der Kampf*.

   In the event, the Austro-Marxists and the Austrian socialist party
(SPÖ) never had the opportunity to implement their economic
plans for the country as a whole, but in Vienna, where the socialists
were in power until 1934, another aspect of socialist planning was
evident in their achievements in providing working-class housing,
health and welfare services, and cultural facilities, and in bringing
about major educational reforms (Bauer 1923, Gulick 1948, vol. 1,
chs 10, 13–16, 18). This was important in giving prominence to an
essential element in socialist planning; namely, the organization of
production to satisfy basic human needs for the whole population,
and a new, more equal division of social welfare. Equally important
was the Austro-Marxist criticism of the course taken by the
Russian Revolution, best expressed by Otto Bauer (1923) in his
book on the Austrian revolution, where he also qualified the idea of
a centrally planned and managed economy through his advocacy of
works' councils:

> Only this self-education in and through the practice of works'
> councils will create the prerequisites for a socialist mode of pro-
> duction. The example of Russia, where the democratic organiza-
> tion of industry which was attempted immediately after the
> October Revolution soon gave way to bureaucratic state
> capitalism, demonstrates that only bureaucratic state socialism –
> which merely replaces the despotism of the employer by the
> despotism of the bureaucrat – is possible so long as the workers

lack the capacity for self-government in the labour process. . . . As
an instrument of proletarian self-government in the production
process the works' councils constitute a preliminary stage of the
socialist mode of production. Consequently, their creation and
development is a more important preparation for a socialist system of society than any forcible act of expropriation, if the results
of the latter are no more than state or municipal undertakings
administered on bureaucratic lines. (p. 166)

Much of the Marxist discussion of a socialist economy in the early
1920s was preoccupied with the question of the role of works'
councils, and more broadly with workers' self-management, in
relation to a centrally planned and managed economy – not only in
Austria, but in Russia (especially through the activities of the
Workers' Opposition, in which Alexandra Kollontai took a leading
part)[1], in Germany, in Czechoslovakia and in Italy (notably in
Gramsci's articles on the Turin factory councils) – and the discussion has revived vigorously in recent years. But from the mid-
1920s to the 1930s Marxist theory came to be dominated partly by
the controversies in the Soviet Union and their repercussions
elsewhere, partly by the 'calculation debate' provoked by anti-
socialist critics.

The influence exerted by the controversies among Soviet
Marxists was theoretically unfortunate in the sense that they had
less to do with the construction of a socialist economy than with the
industrialization of a backward, overwhelmingly agrarian society.
A more extended analysis of the development of the Soviet
economy, and of the historical circumstances which affected it, will
be given in the next chapter, and in the present context I shall
consider only the principal theoretical ideas which emerged. The
'industrialization debate' took place between 1924 and 1928,[2] and
the main protagonists were Bukharin and Preobrazhensky, though
many other leading economists also took part (Erlich 1960, chs 1
and 2). Bukharin, who had fervently supported the economic policy
of 'War Communism', involving the extension of nationalization
and direct control of the whole economy, and presented a theoretical justification of it in his *Economics of the Transformation Period*
(1920), changed his views radically after the introduction of the
New Economic Policy (NEP) which Lenin persuaded the party to
adopt at the end of the civil war and foreign intervention, as a

means of restoring the shattered economy. In a series of articles
from the end of 1924 Bukharin now advocated, for the agricultural
sector of the economy, a liberalization of trade and a relaxation of
the restrictions on hiring labour, but at the same time a strong
effort to promote peasant cooperatives. In the interim, he argued,
'We have to tell the peasantry, all its strata: get rich, accumulate,
develop your economy', since this, along with a liberalization of
foreign trade, would have a stimulating effect on the development
of industry and industrial investment, and would make possible a
reduction in industrial prices. These policies as a whole, Bukharin
argued, would promote general economic growth.

Preobrazhensky (1926), on the other hand, emphasized the
importance of rapid industrialization to overcome the 'goods
famine' and to absorb the surplus agrarian population; he noted
that this must take place on the 'new technological basis' which
required an ever increasing amount of capital per worker. But this
posed a massive problem of accumulation, and the crucial part of
Preobrazhensky's work was his formulation of a 'law of primitive
socialist accumulation' (by analogy with Marx's description of
'primitive capitalist accumulation' in the early stages of the development of capitalism), which involved the suppression of the 'law of
value' governing competitive markets and the imposition of 'forced
saving' on the peasantry, mainly through monopoly pricing by the
state. But Preobrazhensky introduced several qualifications into his
argument, recognizing that the policies he advocated faced major
problems and contradictions, not least the danger of a 'peasants'
strike'; and in a later statement of his position he concluded that
'the sum total of these contradictions shows how strongly our
development toward socialism is confronted with the necessity of
ending our socialist isolation, not only for political but also for
economic reasons, and of leaning for support in the future on the
material resources of other socialist countries' (Erlich 1960, pp. 55–
9). What Preobrazhensky did not foresee, as he acknowledged in
his speech to the seventeenth party congress in 1934, where he also
renounced his law of primitive socialist accumulation as 'a crude
analogy with the epoch of primitive capitalist accumulation', was
the forced collectivization of the peasantry carried out by Stalin, as
a means of accumulating the resources for rapid industrialization
(Nove 1969, p. 220).

The industrialization debate involved a complex of economic and political issues such as Marxists in Western Europe, beginning with Marx himself, had never expected to confront: the industrialization of a backward economy and the construction of 'socialism in one country'; the maintenance of working-class dominance and Bolshevik rule in a society which had three million industrial workers and eighty million peasants; the constant threat, or fear, of military intervention by the capitalist powers. Hence, a considerable gulf emerged between the preoccupations of Soviet Marxists and those in the West, and this was widened by the division in the international working-class movement between the old social democratic parties and the new communist parties. For the most part the social democratic Marxists remained critical of Soviet policies, and especially of the political dictatorship, and conceived the advent of socialism as the outcome of a 'slow revolution' in which, according to Hilferding, organized capitalism would gradually be transformed into socialism as the democratic state took possession of the 'commanding heights' of the economy. Few of them undertook an analysis in any detail of the development of the Soviet economy, or its fundamental problems; one such attempt, by Friedrich Pollock (1929), which was described by a Soviet reviewer as having 'an outstanding place in the ocean of literature on the USSR and its economy',[3] was in fact a largely descriptive account of the system of central planning, while the theoretical discussion which Pollock promised for a later volume never appeared.

It was, however, the implementation of a central plan, which had its first beginnings in the same year (1921) as the introduction of NEP, with the creation of the State Planning Commission ('Gosplan'), that mainly interested socialists elsewhere, and from this aspect there was not such a great difference between the concerns of Western Marxists and Soviet Marxists. But the former found themselves increasingly involved in a theoretical defence of the possibility of central planning in an advanced industrial economy, against the criticisms of anti-socialist economists such as Mises and Hayek; this 'socialist calculation debate' of the 1920s and 1930s, and its prolongation in more recent controversies, will be discussed in Chapter 4. Here, it should be noted that the external conditions of the debate changed dramatically between the end of the 1920s and the mid-1940s, in the first place as a result of the profound economic depression in the capitalist countries, which was interpreted by many Marxists as a 'final crisis' preceding the collapse of capitalism, and in sharp contrast the ruthless collectivization of agriculture and rapid industrialization in the USSR, which made possible its victory in the Second World War and its post-war emergence as an industrial and military superpower. Second, the outcome of the war was an expansion of the Soviet form of socialism into Eastern Europe, a strong Soviet influence on the development of socialism in China and in some Third World countries, and in Western Europe a considerable extension of public ownership, increased state intervention in the economy, and an apparent movement towards democratic socialism, though this was soon checked by a vigorous revival of capitalism aided by the Marshall Plan.

By the end of the 1940s Marxist conceptions of a socialist economy had settled fairly clearly into a pattern in which central planning and state ownership and management of a wide range of industrial enterprises and financial institutions held pride of place; but this began to change in the 1950s. In Yugoslavia the system of workers' self-management was introduced, and a 'socialist market economy' emerged. Then, very gradually, the highly centralized economies in other East European countries began to change, and the process of decentralization and development of a controlled market economy has accelerated rapidly in the past decade. Marxist conceptions of a socialist economy have now become quite diverse and it is very evident at present that no single view holds a clearly dominant position. The more recent debates and schools of thought will be discussed in later chapters, following an examination in the next two chapters of the various forms of socialist planning since the First World War, and the arguments against planning which have been propounded by anti-socialist critics.

Notes

1. See Porter (1980), ch. 16, and the references given there.
2. On this debate see Erlich (1960) and Spulber (1964). Several students of this period have noted that the Soviet economic debates were pioneering attempts in the field of development economics which only much later, after 1945, with the emergence of 'developing countries' and the universal concern with economic growth, engaged the full attention of Western economists. As Spulber (1964, pp. v–vi) notes:

Since the 1950s, which saw the emergence of many newly independent
countries bent on rapid economic growth, preoccupation with massive state
intervention in the economy, forced industrialization, and planning has
given rise in the West to a whole body of literature on economic development. Many of the problems under discussion in this literature and in the
newly developing countries were already confronting Russia in the
1920s. . . . The truth is that the Soviet mid-1920s were teeming with interesting and valuable ideas.

And as other writers have observed, these ideas, and the Soviet
experience of planned industrialization, became in varying degrees a
model or point of reference for the policies of many developing
countries after 1945.
3. Cited in the editorial introduction to the 1971 reprint of Pollock's book.

3

The experience of planning since the First World War

The first socialist planned economy was created in Russia after the revolution of October 1917. It could hardly have appeared in less favourable circumstances, in a predominantly agrarian and backward society, debilitated by three years of war and then by civil war and foreign intervention. The Bolshevik leaders themselves, at least up to the mid-1920s, were doubtful about their ability to retain power, and still more about the possibility of constructing a socialist society without external support from a socialist revolution in one or more of the advanced industrial countries of Western Europe. In the event, as the revolutionary wave in Europe subsided or was quelled, they were forced into the policy of 'building socialism in one country', which required above all massive and rapid industrialization.

The earlier period of Soviet economic development has been well documented in numerous studies,[1] and here I shall only briefly summarize the principal stages. The first stage, that of 'War Communism', was largely determined by the civil war, foreign intervention and the resulting chaotic condition of society. As Nove (1969, p. 47) remarks, 'all the events of 1917–21 were, naturally, dominated by the war and civil war, by destruction and fighting, by depleted supplies and paralysed transport, by the needs of the front and priorities of battle, and last but not least by the loss of vital industrial and agricultural areas to various enemies'. Following the nationalization and redistribution of land, and a brief period of workers' control, state ownership and control of industry and financial institutions were rapidly extended, along with a ban on private trade, and the whole economy moved towards an economy in kind, a moneyless economy – in large measure no doubt as a consequence of the civil war and the prevailing disorder, but also theoretically justified and advocated by Bukharin (1920) and others.[2]

By 1921 industrial production had fallen to about one-third, agricultural output to less than two-thirds, of the 1913 level, and foreign trade had virtually collapsed. At this stage, and particularly after a series of peasant risings and the Kronstadt sailors' revolt of March 1921, Lenin concluded that a major change in economic policy was necessary, the first step being the replacement of the confiscation of peasant surpluses by a food tax in kind (later, in 1924, a money tax) which was set at a lower level than the previous requisitions. The peasants became free to trade as they wished with the rest of their produce, private trade was legalized and then expanded rapidly, along with a strong revival of private manufacturing. This New Economic Policy (NEP), as it came to be called, was 'a form of mixed economy, with an overwhelmingly private agriculture, plus legalized private trade and small-scale private manufacturing' (Nove 1969, p. 86). But at the same time, in 1921, a State Bank was established, which together with the Commissariat of Finance eventually succeeded in ending the massive inflation, and stabilizing the currency, a central planning commission ('Gosplan') was created, and there was a steady expansion of state trusts in manufacturing and trade. By 1925 both industrial and agricultural production were recovering rapidly.

This, however, as Preobrazhensky (1926) noted, was only a restoration of the pre-war level of the economy, achieved by the consumption of fixed capital and stocks of raw material; in his view the possibilities for rationalizing production within the framework of the old technology were 'approaching exhaustion'. The urgent need now was for a programme of industrialization at the new level, made possible by rapid technological progress, which involved a higher amount of fixed capital per worker, and a growth of productive capacity to meet the increased effective demand of the peasantry (Erlich 1960, pp. 32–6). The 'industrialization debate', which was considered in the previous chapter, concerned policies and methods, not the goal of rapid industrialization which was

universally accepted, on both political and economic grounds.
The political considerations were twofold. In the first place, the
civil war and foreign intervention had only recently ended, the
Soviet Union was still encircled by hostile capitalist powers, and
one major aspect of economic planning necessarily related to
military defence. Nove (1969, p. 133) refers to one well-known
example:

> A 'strategic' decision, much discussed at the time, concerned the
> so-called Ural-Kuznetsk combine [actually begun in 1930]. This
> was an immense project linking the iron ore of the Urals with the
> excellent coking coal of the Kuzbas, a thousand miles away in
> Central Siberia. It was a long-term project *par excellence*. It
> would lock up a great deal of capital. It could not be justified by
> rate-of-return calculations. It might have vast external effects in
> the long run. It would – it did – save the situation militarily in the
> event of invasion by 'imperialist' powers.

In a speech delivered in February 1931 to leading personnel of
socialist industry, Stalin (1955, p. 41) observed: 'We are fifty or a
hundred years behind the advanced countries. We must make good
this distance in ten years. Either we do it, or we shall go under'. It
was an astonishingly accurate prediction. The forced industrialization undertaken in the 1930s was a major factor enabling the Soviet
Union to withstand, and eventually turn back, the massive assault
by Nazi Germany in 1941, which involved for the rest of the war
four-fifths of the whole German armed forces.

The second political element in the industrialization programme
concerned the relation between classes. The Bolsheviks had led a
successful 'proletarian revolution' based upon a very small industrial working class in alliance with a very large peasantry, and it was
apparent to all of them that the existence of millions of peasant
households engaged in independent production, along with the
growth of private small-scale manufacture and private trade during
the NEP period, continually recreated the conditions for a revival
of capitalism and constituted a threat to the development of a
socialist society, even though, as Bukharin argued, the Bolsheviks
continued to occupy the 'commanding heights' of the economy.
Industrialization, therefore, was also seen as crucial in changing the
balance of social forces by enlarging the industrial working class

and increasing its political weight. The policy of forced industrialization which began with the First Five Year Plan in 1928
was then complemented by the forced collectivization of agriculture
to eliminate, or at least severely restrict, independent peasant
production.

Finally, the purely economic consequences of rapid industrialization were essential to achieving the social aims of a socialist society
by raising living standards, ensuring full employment, and expand-
ing the social services; all of which depended upon sustained
economic growth. In these respects the development of the Soviet
Union in the 1930s contrasted strongly with conditions in the
capitalist world – to such an extent that the Webbs (1935)
concluded their generally very favourable account of the Soviet
Union as 'a new civilization' by saying that this civilization had
been successful and was likely to spread elsewhere.[3]

There had, of course, been some extension of economic and
social planning in the European capitalist countries after the First
World War. The war economy accustomed people to much more
extensive state intervention and regulation of production, and there
were many who considered that this experience would lead
gradually towards a socialist system.[4] Initially, too, the Russian
Revolution gave a further impetus to the socialist movement, and
several revolutionary upheavals in central Europe instituted for
brief periods agencies and measures of state planning, notably in
Hungary and Bavaria (where Neurath, as I have noted, played a
prominent part). With the defeat of the revolutionary movements,
however, very little in the way of socialist planning survived outside
the Soviet Union. Nevertheless, the ideas of extended state
intervention, public ownership and central planning remained
potent, and on a limited scale effective. In most European countries
state intervention in the economy did gradually increase, mainly
through the growth of expenditure on welfare services (unemployment benefits, old age pensions, low-cost housing),[5] and at a local
level, in municipalities and districts, some elements of socialist
policies could be implemented.[6] But there was little or no extension
of public ownership[7] and no agencies for comprehensive national
planning were created.

The greatest change came with the economic depression that
began in 1929. In the first place this gave a new vigour to the
socialist criticisms of capitalism, and to the advocacy of a planned

economy to deal with mass unemployment and poverty. A considerable literature on planning developed, well exemplified in Britain by the writings of Wootton and Durbin. Wootton (1934) first examined the Soviet planned economy, then made a fairly detailed comparison between planned and unplanned economies, and concluded with a discussion of 'the conditions of successful economic planning', in which she emphasized as the first prerequisite 'knowledge and the ability to use that knowledge' (p. 303), which in turn required the creation of a general planning commission able to 'draw up plans and to supervise their execution' (p. 307). She then went on to consider some 'difficult questions' of socialist planning, such as the degree of dependence on, or independence of, a price mechanism, and the role of economic motives in a socialist society.[8]

Durbin, in his essay on 'the importance of planning' (1935, republished with later essays on planning in Durbin 1949), observed that 'it would be almost true to say that "we are all *Planners* now". The collapse of the popular faith in *laissez-faire* has proceeded with spectacular rapidity in this country and all over the world since the War' (p. 41). But he then distinguished two kinds of planning: (a) as 'meaning simply the *intervention of the Government in a particular industry* at a time when the greater part of the economy still remains in private hands', and (b) that 'which results in the *general supersession of individual enterprise* as the source of economic decisions' (p. 42). In his later discussion he rejected the idea of rigid long-term plans which could not be quickly amended to take account of changes in human tastes, technical inventions and so on, and defined planning generally as an 'extension of the size of the unit of management and the consequent enlargement of the field surveyed when any economic decision is taken' (p. 44). Durbin then considered the aims of socialist planning, replied to some major criticisms of planning (which I shall examine in the next chapter), emphasized the importance of centralized monetary control, and sketched the institutions necessary for democratic socialist planning.

A Marxist study, *Britain Without Capitalists* (1936), presented a sustained criticism of the capitalist organization of the economy and outlined an economic system for a 'Soviet Britain', taking as its explicit model the Soviet economy. After considering the economy as a whole the authors undertook a detailed examination of the major sectors of economic activity and concluded with a chapter on science and education which is still illuminating for the way in which it argues the need for reform and expansion (still today, in Britain, only partially achieved). The book attracted quite widespread attention even from defenders of the status quo,[9] and was a notable addition to the literature which began to create a climate of opinion more favourable to planning.

From this aspect it also illustrated a second consequence of the economic depression: namely, an increasing awareness of the sharp contrast between the economic conditions in the capitalist countries and in the Soviet Union. While the former seemed to be in decline, the Soviet Union appeared to be making (and as we now know, was in fact making, in many spheres) rapid progress, and came to be regarded by many people, not only those who were its committed supporters, as a viable and hopeful alternative to capitalism. Both Wootton and the Webbs undertook a close study of the Soviet economy, and the latter, as we have seen, concluded that this 'new civilization' would spread elsewhere. It was undoubtedly the economic conditions and contrasts of the 1930s which provided the stimulus for the growth of the socialist and communist parties in many of the European capitalist countries, to an extent that became very evident in the years immediately following the Second World War.

In fact, the pressure exerted by the growing socialist movement was making itself felt already in the 1930s, and there was an increase in planning in several countries. One notable example is Sweden, where the Social Democratic Labour Party (SAP) came to power in 1932, and has been almost continuously in power ever since. Social democratic rule has not brought extensive public ownership, but it has greatly increased public sector spending and the degree of state intervention in the economy, creating gradually a very advanced form of 'welfare state'; and more recently the sphere of public ownership has begun to be enlarged in an original way, which will be discussed in a later chapter, through the development of employee investment funds.

Elsewhere there was also a general growth of state intervention and partial planning, in a variety of forms. In the United States the New Deal, as Roosevelt had indicated in his inaugural address in March 1933, involved an extension of state intervention, first in a reform of the banking system then in a rationalization of industry, initially through the National Industrial Recovery Act; a reorganization of agriculture (which included, as the boldest measure of the New Deal experiment, the creation of a large public corporation, the Tennessee Valley Authority); and an ambitious programme of relief for the unemployed carried out mainly by the Works Progress Administration, which spent vast sums of money on public works of all kinds. In Britain, on a much smaller and less imaginative scale, state intervention also increased, mainly in the form of measures to rationalize agriculture and some industries (notably iron and steel) and the provision of subsidies (for example, to shipping).

This trend towards greater state intervention and regulation, and partial planning, at least in the sense of rationalization,[10] gained momentum with the approach of the Second World War. Indeed it was only later in the 1930s, as the war loomed and rearmament programmes were undertaken, that unemployment began to decline significantly in many of the capitalist countries. Germany, after 1933, had what was virtually a war economy, and from the mid-1930s other countries embarked upon more gradual and limited rearmament, which involved an extension of state intervention and planning. The war itself brought massive state regulation of the economy, from the outset, on an even larger scale than during the First World War, and raised similar expectations that many aspects of economic and social planning would be continued in the post-war period, creating conditions favourable to the gradual construction of a socialist economy and form of society in the European countries.

In Britain, the advent of a Labour government in 1945 made possible an extension of public ownership by the nationalization of some major industries, and an expansion of social services, notably through the creation of a national health service. Elsewhere, as a result of particular circumstances, there was also an extension of public ownership; in France, where enterprises owned by collaborators with the German occupation forces were nationalized, and in Austria, where many enterprises which were German property during the period of Austria's incorporation in the Third Reich were confiscated by the Allied occupying forces and then remained in public ownership when they were returned to Austria between 1946 and 1955. In Germany itself the policy of 'co-determination' created an element of workers' participation in the management of privately owned enterprises, and generally increased the influence of the trade unions and the Social Democratic Party.[11]

The war also extended socialist planning more directly by establishing the dominance of the Soviet Union in Eastern Europe, where new socialist economies were created on the Soviet model.[12] One of these countries, Yugoslavia, soon separated itself from the rest of Eastern Europe, however, and pursued an independent course of development by introducing workers' self-management and an early form of 'socialist market economy'.[13] But the Soviet model was also followed by many of the newly independent countries of the Third World as they embarked upon programmes designed to establish a modern economic infrastructure and basic industries, and to achieve rapid economic growth.[14]

The experience of planning from the First World War to the years immediately following the Second World War indicates that three different kinds of planning have influenced the development of modern societies. First, there is the planning associated with the war economies of the First and Second World Wars, which, as I have argued, showed the feasibility of planning and also provided practical experience of the operation of planning mechanisms. After both wars planning and state intervention in the economies of the European countries continued at a higher level than during the pre-war period, and this was especially the case after the Second World War, partly because of the extension of planning which had already taken place in the inter-war years to cope with the economic depression, and partly because of the increased strength of the socialist parties and trade unions in Europe at the end of the war.

Second, there is the partial planning, involving rationalization, government subsidies, some public ownership, and in general a greater state involvement in the regulation of the economy, which developed in the capitalist countries (including the United States) during the depression of the 1930s and continued, especially in the West European countries, in the period of reconstruction after the Second World War. This corresponded broadly with what Hilferding (1927) called 'organized capitalism', and what orthodox Marxist-Leninists later referred to as 'state monopoly capitalism'.[15] Subsequently, the notions expressed in these two conceptions of the development of advanced capitalism were merged to some extent in the concept of corporatism, which I shall consider later in this chapter.

Third, there is the comprehensive planning, resting on public ownership of the major means of production, exemplified by the Soviet economy and extended after 1945 to Eastern Europe, as well as being adopted as a model, in greater or lesser degree, by many Third World countries. This kind of comprehensive planning had an important influence, in various ways, on the changes taking place in capitalist countries after 1945. Thus, in Britain the post-war Labour government introduced what Devons (1970, pp. 67–83) referred to as 'planning by economic survey', publishing in 1947 the first annual *Economic Survey*, which had an introductory chapter on economic planning followed by an outline of three sets of plans which the government intended or hoped to implement. Similarly, in some other European countries, more comprehensive types of planning were envisaged and partly implemented.[16] Furthermore, as Tinbergen (1968, p. 102) points out, 'some national planning was imposed on all member countries of the Organization of European Economic Cooperation (OEEC), created to administer the European Recovery, or Marshall, Plan, which started operations in 1948'.

While the war economies do clearly form a very distinct category, in spite of some variations between countries, the categories of 'partial' (or 'capitalist') and 'comprehensive' (or 'socialist') planning should not, in my view, be regarded as absolutely distinct and exclusive. There are, in the predominantly capitalist countries, degrees of planning which may tend, in some countries and during some periods, towards a more socialist form of economy; and on the other side it is increasingly evident that comprehensively planned socialist societies may undergo modification by the introduction of market mechanisms and an enlargement of the sphere of private enterprise, while the major part of economic production remains firmly in the public sector.

The rest of this chapter will be devoted to an examination of the experience of, and experiments in, socialist planning since the end of the Second World War. Before embarking on that, however, it is necessary to make a further comment on the general notion of planning, which cannot and should not be limited simply to economic planning in the strict sense. All the diverse forms of planning and state intervention, in capitalist and socialist societies, as they have developed since the First World War, involve both economic and social planning; and socialist planning which is directed, as I argued in the introduction to this book, towards the creation of a new type of society, necessarily gives an exceptional importance to the provision for all citizens, on a basis of equality, of those services which enhance the quality of life – among which the most fundamental are adequate housing, universal health care and education, efficient public transport and communication, cultural and recreational facilities, and protection of the physical environment. As we shall see, socialist policies have indeed emphasized these aspects of planning (except that environmental protection has only recently become a prominent concern), and can show major achievements in most of these fields.

Let us begin by considering the planned economies of the Soviet Union and the countries of Eastern Europe. It is generally acknowledged that the rapid industrialization of the 1930s was the crucial factor enabling the Soviet Union to emerge victorious from the Second World War as a major industrial power, though it may be questioned whether quite such breakneck speed in the development of industry and the related collectivization of agriculture was necessary, and still more whether it had to be undertaken with the brutality that Stalin imparted to the whole process (Nove 1964). Erlich (1960, pp. xx–xxi) sums up the achievement by saying that 'The Soviet economic advance since 1928 has been one of the dominant facts of our time. . . . According to the virtually unanimous view of Western students, the expansion of the Soviet industrial capacity has proceeded at a rate which is, by any meaningful standard of comparison, unprecedented.' The exceptionally high rate of economic growth was resumed after the war, in the period 1950–8, but it has steadily declined since then, and particularly sharply since the mid-1970s; furthermore, the annual rate of growth has always been very much lower in agriculture, averaging only about 3 per cent compared with 6 or 7 per cent in industry.[17]

In the new socialist countries after 1945 the imposition of a Stalinist type of planning led to the same massive concentration of effort on rapid industrialization as in the earlier period in the Soviet Union, at the cost of severely restricting consumption in favour of investment, and establishing dictatorial and repressive regimes.[18] This planned industrialization was, for the most part, effectively carried out (most successfully in Czechoslovakia and the German Democratic Republic) and as Wilczynski (1982, p. 215) comments, the share of the European socialist countries (including the Soviet Union) in world industrial output:

> . . . increased from less than 10 per cent in 1938 to about 30 per cent in 1970, and in 1978 it was about 31 per cent (but, according to some Socialist estimates, it was 37 per cent). In the leading Western nations basic industrialization took some twenty-five to fifty years to achieve, but in the European Socialist countries this process was completed in twelve to twenty years. In view of the semi-feudal conditions that they inherited, the absence of colonies, the widespread wartime devastation, western boycotts and the strategic embargo and practically no aid from the capitalist world, their achievements can be described by objective observers as spectacular.

This uniform type of planning did not, however, persist for very long. Yugoslavia withdrew from the Soviet orbit in 1948 and began to develop its own system of workers' self-management, and Soviet influence in China diminished from the mid-1950s as that country too embarked on a distinctive course of socialist development. In the Soviet Union and the East European countries changes in the economic system began to be made after the death of Stalin, and the need for change became more widely recognized as a consequence of the slowing down of economic growth in the late 1950s and a succession of revolts against the political rulers in several countries from 1953 to 1980. The main features of this process of change are the reorientation of production towards increasing the supply of consumer goods, and more fundamentally, a reconstruction of the whole economic system involving decentralization and the development of elements of a market economy.

In the past decade, and especially since the accession to power of Mr Gorbachev in the Soviet Union, the speed of change has greatly increased, and in later chapters the major forms and projects of reconstruction will be examined more closely. Here it will suffice to make some general observations on the experience of socialist planning thus far. The European socialist countries have become major industrial producers (China will undoubtedly reach the same position within a relatively short time), and the per capita GDP of most of them probably lies within the range of 85 per cent to 125 per cent of that in the United Kingdom (Wilczynski 1982, p. 212). Hence those early criticisms of central planning, which declared that it would prove impossible to carry out and that the Soviet economy would simply collapse, were, as we shall see in the next chapter, very wide of the mark.

The slowing down of economic growth since the 1960s, and more particularly since the mid-1970s, may be explained in part by the maturation of the socialist countries as industrial societies. The high rates of growth in the earlier stages, on this view, reflected the rapid industralization from a low initial level, and many economists have suggested that their growth rates will eventually settle at the levels characteristic of the advanced capitalist countries (though perhaps without the same degree of cyclical fluctuation); but socialist economists have generally disputed this view, arguing that a socialist planned economy makes it possible to sustain higher average growth rates over the longer term.

There is, however, another factor to be considered in evaluating the recent decline in growth rates and the prospects for the future. Economic growth in the socialist countries until the last decade was mainly *extensive*, that is to say, achieved by bringing into production additional quantities of land, labour and capital, whereas in advanced industrial societies it has become increasingly *intensive*, brought about by technological progress. The need for development based upon the application of new technology was, of course, strongly emphasized by Preobrazhensky in the industrialization debate of the 1920s – as I noted in the previous chapter – and more recently by Richta and his colleagues (1969), who argued, starting out from Marx's conception in the *Grundrisse* of an advanced modern society in which scientific knowledge and its application has become the major productive force, that intensive growth would be more effectively promoted in the centrally planned socialist economies than in capitalist economies.[19] The preoccupation with intensive growth in the European socialist countries is illustrated by the prominence given to the use of the term 'scientific and technological revolution' in much social science research and writing over the past decade.[20] Yet, in practice, technological progress seems to have lagged behind that in most of the major capitalist countries (except probably in the Soviet space programme and in defence), notwithstanding the large resources devoted to science and technology; and the current reforms in the Soviet Union and other socialist countries are largely designed to give a fresh stimulus to economic growth by encouraging innovation and enterprise (Berliner 1988, chs. 9, 11 and 12).

One other aspect of socialist planning, which will be discussed more fully later, should be mentioned briefly at this point. As I have emphasized from the outset, socialist economic planning is not an end in itself, but is intended to establish the basis of a socialist society, in which the benefits (material and cultural) of rising levels of production are distributed as widely and equally among the population as the general conditions of the time permit. Above all, this has meant in the socialist countries the maintenance of full employment, the eradication of illiteracy and a rapid development of the whole educational system, the provision of free, or very low-cost services in many spheres (housing, public transport, recreational and cultural facilities) and the expansion of health and welfare services. In their study of social welfare in the Soviet Union, which I cited in the introduction, George and Manning (1980, pp. 167–8) observe that the intentions of social policy there are more comprehensive and ambitious than in any welfare capitalist society,[21] though the achievements may not always match the aims, largely because of economic constraints. I also cited in the introduction the study of Third World socialist countries by White, Murray and White (1983) which shows that these countries have been much more successful than non-socialist developing countries in eradicating illiteracy and extending health services to the mass of the population, while attaining broadly comparable rates of economic growth.

After the Second World War, planning, including some elements of socialist planning, was also considerably extended in many advanced capitalist countries. In part this was an outcome of wartime planning and the need for post-war reconstruction (as after the First World War); but it was due much more to the growth of the socialist movement in Western Europe, to the still vivid memories of the pre-war depression and the desire to regulate the economy in such a way that these conditions would not recur, and in a lesser degree to the example of Soviet planning, which had become more widely known and influential in the 1930s and during the wartime alliance (though this proved to be a short-lived influence, soon destroyed by the Cold War and the ideological redefinition of world politics in terms of a conflict between 'totalitarianism' and the 'free world'). As I noted above, the post-war Labour Government in Britain nationalized some sectors of the economy and proposed to introduce more comprehensive planning, guided by the annual *Economic Survey* (though this never came about), and there were similar nationalizations in other West European countries, though not in the United States or Japan. The extension of public ownership and a higher level of government spending on social welfare greatly enhanced the economic role of the state, and by the mid-1970s state expenditure in the advanced capitalist countries generally ranged between 40 and 50 per cent of the total GDP (though this, of course, included rapidly increasing military expenditure, especially in the United States). In no country, however, did the publicly owned sector dominate the economy as a whole, or in most cases, the crucially important financial institutions; and the economic system that had emerged by the 1970s was often described as 'corporatism' – a form of 'mixed economy' which was managed and regulated by negotiation and agreement between the state, the large capitalist corporations and the trade unions – though Marxists were more inclined to define it as 'organized capitalism' or 'state monopoly capitalism'.

The development of this system in Western Europe represented a precarious balance achieved between the increased strength of the socialist movement and the resurrection of European capitalism through the Marshall Plan and the economic dominance of the United States (Van de Pijl 1989, pp. 254–8). It checked the extension of public ownership and of socialist planning, but at the same time involved much more planning of the economy than in the pre-war period, both in individual countries and on a regional or international level. The 'march into socialism' seemed indeed to have come to a halt at that 'halfway house' which Schumpeter (1987, p. 422) envisaged as a possible sticking point.

Yet the spread of planning is quite evident in many countries. In France, for example, a decree of January 1946 provided for 'a first overall modernization and investment plan for metropolitan France and the overseas territories', and set up planning machinery in the form of a *Conseil du Plan* and a *Commissariat Général* (Seibel 1975, p. 153). This undoubtedly played a major part in French recovery and subsequent economic growth, in striking contrast with Britain where no effective central planning machinery was ever established.[22] By 1975, however, conditions in France had changed, and as Seibel (*ibid.*) indicates:

. . . forecasting methods have improved, the scope of planning has widened, and planning machinery has become more prominent in government departments – but the plan itself has become less and less imperative, and also more difficult to formulate. . . . What started out as the 'Nation's Plan' became a 'medium-term government programme'. . . .

Nevertheless, the existence of this machinery and the experience of planning facilitated some resumption of national planning by socialist governments in the 1980s, as well as influencing planning in the European Community (EC).

Another example of very successful post-war planning is to be found in Japan, where national economic plans have been prepared by the Economic Planning Agency every two or three years from 1955 (Komiya 1975, p. 189). Komiya, however, argues that these national plans are not as important as may appear at first, and much planning takes place in other ways. 'The Japanese government intervenes widely in individual sectors, industries, or regions . . .' (*ibid.*), especially through the government offices called *genkyoku*, each of which supervises a particular industry and is responsible for policies concerning the industry (*ibid.*, pp. 209–10).[23]

Planning in the capitalist countries differs considerably, of course, from that in socialist countries, where the plans are more comprehensive, more imperative than indicative, and involve direct state management of a large part of the economy, as well as having somewhat different objectives insofar as a high priority is given to maintaining full employment and to the provision of welfare services. Nevertheless, there is some convergence, through the socialist influence – particularly strong in some countries – on capitalist planning and more recently through changes in the economic systems of the European socialist countries. What is unmistakable is that large-scale planning, in one form or another, has become vastly more important in the advanced industrial countries and that it has produced some impressive results. Tinbergen (1968, p. 109) concludes his discussion of economic planning in Western Europe by saying that

planning has succeeded in avoiding the main inconsistency in unplanned economies of the pre-1914 type, namely, the underutilization of productive capacity as a consequence of business cycles and of structural disequilibria. It is highly probable that the disappearance of the business cycle after World War II has been obtained with the aid of macroeconomic planning of the type described in this article.

It may be added that the growth of the West European economies after 1945, with more extensive planning and much greater state intervention, was more rapid and stable than in any other period of modern history, with a growth rate more than twice as high as that of the period 1918–38 (Postan 1967, ch. 1). In the European socialist countries, as I have noted, the rate of growth was even higher, and in the face of great difficulties most of these countries developed with remarkable speed the essential foundations of an advanced industrial society.

From this short historical account of the experience of planning we can reach, I think, some initial tentative conclusions: first, that a trend towards economic and social planning established itself in the 1930s and became much stronger after the Second World War; and second, that this extension of planning had a very successful outcome in a marked acceleration of economic growth and the creation of 'welfare states' in much of the capitalist world. The success of planning may also be judged from the other side by observing that the two least-planned capitalist societies – Britain and the United States – are those which at present confront the greatest economic difficulties and show most clearly the symptoms of decline. At the same time, the comprehensively planned socialist societies have also encountered serious problems and are now engaged in a radical restructuring of their economies. We have next to consider, therefore, the major criticisms of planning, especially socialist planning, before proceeding to a more detailed study of the economic institutions and political framework of a socialist society in the light of recent changes in ideas and practice.

Notes

1. Besides the works by Pollock (1929), Erlich (1960) and Nove (1969), mentioned in the previous chapter, see Dobb (1928) and Carr (1952).

2. See Nove (1969, ch. 3). As was noted in the previous chapter, Neurath was also advocating at this time an economy in kind.
3. S. and B. Webb (1935, p. 1143): 'Will this new civilization with its abandonment of profit-making, its extinction of unemployment, its planned production for community consumption . . . spread to other countries? Our own reply is: "Yes, it will". But how, when, where, with what modifications, and whether through violent revolution or by peaceful penetration, or even by conscious imitation, are questions we cannot answer'.
4. This was the case with many of the Austro-Marxists (see above p. 23) and also, for example, the British Labour Party whose post-war reconstruction programme, *Labour and the New Social Order*, was based on the assumption (erroneous as it turned out) that the wartime collectivism was unlikely to be abandoned whatever government came to power. But there were many who contested the likelihood of a development towards socialism on the basis of wartime experience. Thus Max Weber (1918) argued that while 'a gradual elimination of private capitalism is theoretically possible – even though it is not such a trifling matter as many *literati*, who do not know anything about it, dream – it will certainly not be brought about by this war'; and he went on to claim that even if it were achieved, far from liberating the worker it would make him still more dependent on the new bureaucratic controllers of the means of production.
5. In Britain, for example, government expenditure as a proportion of GDP rose from about 10 per cent before 1914 to about 20 per cent in the 1930s, and there was a similar trend in other countries.
6. A particularly good example is the socialist administration of Vienna (see p. 27) above.
7. The expectation, in Britain, that the coal mines and the railways were destined for nationalization proved illusory; in Germany, the work of the various Socialization Commissions established during the period immediately following the end of the war achieved nothing; and elsewhere in Europe there was no significant or enduring shift from private to public ownership.
8. Wootton's excellent book provides a model in many respects for a new comparative study, in the very different conditions of the present time, of planned and unplanned economies, as well as material for the kind of large-scale study, which I think has never been attempted though it is greatly to be desired, of the history and sociology of planning. Another good example of the literature on planning is provided by the broadsheets published from April 1933, under the title *Planning*, by a group of people concerned about the economic difficulties of the depression and the need for 'reconstruction' of the British economy.

9. The *Financial News* described it as 'decidely stimulating. . . . For defenders of the existing social system the book is likely to prove one of the finest tonics that has come their way for a long time'.
10. There is a good critical discussion of capitalist rationalization in Bauer (1931).
11. Many studies of economic planning in individual countries of Western Europe were published in the 1960s, and there is also a brief general study by Tinbergen (1968) which lists some of the principal references. See also the discussion by Myrdal (1960).
12. For a brief general survey see Montias (1968).
13. There is a good general account and discussion of the Yugoslav system up to the end of the 1960s in Broekmeyer (1970).
14. The Soviet model, however, was misleading in certain respects, since the undoubted success of Soviet industrialization depended upon several factors — the existence of an advanced industrial sector, though on a small scale, before the revolution, the unchallenged political dominance of a disciplined revolutionary party, and the possession of substantial natural resources in a large territory – which were absent in most of the developing countries. Only in the larger countries was the Soviet experience valuable as a model of economic development – in India (to some extent, and in a diluted form) and in China (with many subsequent modifications).
15. See Wirth (1972) and the critical evaluations by Hardach and Karras (1978) and Jessop (1982).
16. On France, see Fourastié and Courthéoux (1963); on Norway, see Bjerve (1959).
17. Estimates of economic growth in the USSR and East European socialist countries vary considerably between the official figures and those produced by Western economists. The diverse estimates are discussed by Wilczynski (1982, pp. 53–6) and the figures given in the text broadly follow his conclusions. Buck and Cole (1987, ch. 8) suggest rather lower rates of growth in the Soviet economy, but nevertheless point out that the Soviet growth rate has been higher, and more stable, than that of the United States. However, it has not been significantly higher than the growth rate of some West European countries, and is considerably lower than that of Japan.
18. There were, of course, substantial differences between countries; Czechoslovakia already had an important modern industrial sector and the German Democratic Republic, which had formed part of an advanced industrial society, was in a very favourable situation for rapid industrial growth. These two countries, the most prosperous in Eastern Europe, had both attained by the late 1970s a per capita GDP higher than that of the United Kingdom (Wilczynski 1982, p. 212).

19. In discussing Marx's *Grundrisse* elsewhere (Bottomore 1988, pp. 19–21) I have suggested that his vision of the future society might be expressed by adding to his well-known aphorism, 'The hand mill gives you a society with the feudal lord, the steam mill a society with the industrial capitalist', the phrase: 'The automated mill gives you a classless society'; this seems to be the sense in which Richta and others understand the significance of technological progress. At all events it can be said that automated production and modern information technology make central planning a great deal easier and in principle more effective.

20. See for example the contributions by Fedoseyev and Richta to *Scientific-Technological Revolution: Social Aspects* (1977).

21. By 'welfare capitalist societies' is meant primarily the societies of Western Europe and some Commonwealth countries (Australia, Canada, New Zealand). The term does not apply, in any comprehensive sense, to Japan or the United States. Furthermore, there is now a tendency to erode the welfare state in some West European countries, notably in Britain.

22. The contrast was examined in an issue of *Planning* (vol. 29, no. 475, 9 September 1963) on 'French planning: some lessons for Britain', which expressed 'the concern felt about the low rate of growth in the British economy during the 1950s, and an increasing awareness that some sort of planning will be a necessary element in any policy adopted to remedy this situation. The French system of four-year plans provides a working example of the type of planning that could be used in Britain . . .'.

23. See also Morioka (1989, pp. 150–4) and Dore (1987, Introduction).

4

Critiques of socialist planning

The criticisms of socialist planning – and by extension, of the more limited types of planning in capitalist societies – fall into two main categories: those concerning rational calculation in a planned economy, and those concerning bureaucracy, management, incentives and related questions. I shall discuss first the issues that were raised in the notorious 'socialist calculation debate' of the 1930s. The ground of this debate was established earlier, at the turn of the century, by the Austrian marginalist school, but the members of the School differed considerably in their attitudes to socialism;[1] and Wieser in particular, in developing a 'theory of imputation' to determine the value of means of production in any economic system, helped to prepare the way for models of calculation in a planned economy. As Landauer (1959, p. 1624) suggests: 'By elaborating formulae for the determination of the shares of all productive agents in the value of the product, the "Austrian School" laid the ground for the concept of a national accounting system in a socialist society.'[2]

Böhm-Bawerk, on the other hand, was a more hostile critic of socialism, especially Marxist socialism. His criticism rests upon his rejection of the labour theory of value and exploitation in favour of a subjective value theory, expounded in his work on the theory of interest (1884 and later editions) and his essay (1896) on the third volume of Marx's *Capital* (to which Hilferding [1904] wrote a notable reply).[3] The core of his argument was that socialism would not achieve all that socialists hoped for, because it would face similar problems to those in a capitalist economy, arising from the scarcity of resources and time-consuming roundabout methods of production, one consequence of which is that a socialist economy would also require a positive rate of interest. Böhm-Bawerk did not assert, however, that a socialist economy would be unworkable, and it was only later, after the Russian Revolution, that this kind of argument became central, its most fervent and intransigent exponent being Mises.

Indeed it was Mises (1920, 1922) who initiated the 'calculation debate', in which Hayek and Robbins on one side, Lange, Lerner and Dickinson on the other, subsequently participated. The core of his argument was that in a developed complex economy, economic (i.e. monetary) calculation with respect to the production of higher order (production) goods as well as lower order (consumption) goods is only possible in a free market which establishes the exchange value of all goods:

> . . . as soon as one gives up the conception of a freely established monetary price for goods of a higher order, rational production becomes completely impossible. Every step that takes us away from private ownership of the means of production and from the use of money also takes us away from rational economics. (Mises 1920, p. 104)

This argument was elaborated in two directions. First, Mises emphasized that in a free market economy the system of computation by value is employed by every individual member, both as a consumer who establishes a scale of valuation for consumption goods and as a producer who puts goods of a higher order to such use as brings the highest return. But this system, he claimed, 'is necessarily absent from a socialist state', in which the administration can determine what consumption goods are most urgently needed but cannot establish a precise valuation of the means of production. Taking the example of building a new railway, he concluded that the decision, in a socialist society, 'would depend at best upon vague estimates; it would never be based upon the foundation of an exact calculation value' (*ibid.*, pp. 107–9).

Second, Mises drew a contrast between a static condition of society, in which economic calculation might be dispensed with, and a dynamic condition (the real life situation of a modern society), in which economic circumstances are constantly changing and 'we have the spectacle of a socialist economic order floundering in the ocean of possible and conceivable economic combinations without the compass of economic calculation' (*ibid.*, pp. 109–10). His argument concluded with the succinct declaration that 'Where there is no free market, there is no pricing mechanism; without a pricing mechanism, there is no economic calculation' (*ibid.*, p. 111).

In this essay Mises confined himself fairly strictly to economic analysis, but in later writings he broadened the scope of his criticism and was led by his detestation of the whole socialist movement into wild exaggerations, as in the conclusion to his book on socialism (1922, p. 511), where he wrote:

> If the intellectual dominance of Socialism remains unshaken, then in a short time the whole co-operative system of culture which Europe has built up over thousands of years will be shattered. For a socialist order of society is unrealizable. All efforts to realize Socialism lead only to the destruction of society. Factories, mines, and railways will come to a standstill, towns will be deserted. The population of the industrial territories will die out or migrate elsewhere. The farmer will return to the self-sufficiency of the closed, domestic economy. Without private ownership in the means of production there is, in the long run, no production other than a hand-to-mouth production for one's own needs.
>
> We need not describe in detail the cultural and political consequences of such a transformation. Nomad tribes from the Eastern steppes would again raid and pillage Europe, sweeping across it with swift cavalry. Who could resist them in the thinly populated land left defenceless after the weapons inherited from the higher technique of Capitalism had worn out?

The reality, as we have seen, was very different from this fantasy, and it was an important factor in the gradual erosion of the calculation debate itself. Meanwhile, however, a number of socialist economists responded to the critical studies by Mises and others, and propounded a theoretical defence of central planning.

Lange, in the course of his life, proposed several different models of a socialist economy (Kowalik 1987a), but the one for which he is best known is that of market socialism expounded in two articles (1936, 1937) which were then incorporated in a book, with additions and modifications (arising mainly from critical comments by A. P. Lerner), together with an essay by Fred M. Taylor (Lange and Taylor 1938). Lange rejected Mises' main 'contention that a socialist economy cannot solve the problem of rational allocation of its resources' as being 'based on a confusion concerning the nature of prices':

> As Wicksteed has pointed out, the term 'price' has two meanings. It may mean price in the ordinary sense, i.e. the exchange ratio of the two commodities on a market, or it may have the generalized meaning of 'terms on which alternatives are offered'.
> . . . It is only prices in the generalized sense which are indispensable to solving the problem of allocation of resources. . . . To solve the problem three data are needed: (1) a preference scale which guides the acts of choice; (2) knowledge of the 'terms on which alternatives are offered'; and (3) knowledge of the amount of resources available. . . . Now it is obvious that a socialist economy may regard the data under 1 and 3 as given, at least in as great a degree as they are given in a capitalist economy. The data under 1 may either be given by the demand schedules of individuals or be established by the judgment of the authorities administering the economic system. The question remains whether the data under 2 are accessible to the administrators of a socialist economy. Professor Mises denies this. However, a careful study of price theory and of the theory of production convinces us that, the data under 1 and under 3 being given, the 'terms on which alternatives are offered' are determined ultimately by the technical possibilities of transformation of one commodity into another, i.e. by the production functions. The administrators of a socialist economy will have exactly the same knowledge, or lack of knowledge, of the production functions as the capitalist entrepreneurs have. (1938, pp. 59–61)[4]

After discussing what he called the 'more refined form' given to Mises' argument by Hayek and Robbins (to which I shall return later), and the determination of equilibrium on a competitive market, Lange outlined his conception of how a socialist economy would function:

> In the socialist system as described we have a genuine market (in the institutional sense of the word) for consumers' goods and for the services of labour. But there is no market for capital goods

and productive resources outside of labour . . . [and their prices]
are thus prices in the generalized sense, i.e. mere indices of
alternatives available, fixed for accounting purposes. (p. 73)[5]

Lange went on to argue that, 'just as in a competitive individualist
regime', the determination of equilibrium in a socialist system
consists of two parts. First, on the basis of *given* indices of
alternatives (market prices in the cases of consumer goods and
labour services, accounting prices in other cases) both individuals
as consumers and as owners of labour services and the managers of
production (assumed to be public officials), make decisions according to certain principles. Second, both market and accounting
prices are determined by the condition that the quantity of each
commodity demanded is equal to the quantity supplied. There is
also a further condition concerning income distribution, now
divorced from ownership of productive resources (except labour)
and determined in part by social policy. The managers of production are no longer guided by the aim of maximizing profit, but by
rules imposed on them by a Central Planning Board; one rule
requiring the choice of a combination of factors which minimizes
the average cost of production, a second rule (imposed on managers
of individual plants and of whole industries) requiring that output
is fixed so that marginal cost is equal to the price of the product
(pp. 74–6).

Following this discussion of the theoretical determination of
economic equilibrium in a socialist society, Lange considered the
actual formation of prices by a method of trial and error, as
described in Taylor's essay (pp. 51–4), and concluded that 'accounting prices in a socialist economy can be determined by the same
process of trial and error by which prices on a competitive market
are determined' (p. 87). Finally, he reviewed briefly the advantages
and disadvantages of a socialist system. The main advantages are,
first, that 'only a socialist economy can distribute incomes so as to
attain the maximum social welfare', (p. 99), and second, that a
socialist economy would take account of all the alternatives
sacrificed and realized in production, including the social overhead
costs, thus avoiding 'much of the social waste connected with
private enterprise' as well as the fluctuations of the business cycle
(pp. 103–6). Among the disadvantages of socialism he mentioned
the possible arbitrariness of the rate of capital accumulation, and

the problem of the efficiency of public officials compared with private entrepreneurs as managers of production; 'the real danger of socialism', he concluded, 'is that of a bureaucratization of economic life' (p. 109).

After the Second World War, however, Lange became more critical of market socialism and those he called the 'socialist free-marketers' (Kowalik 1987a, p. 128); towards the end of his life he became preoccupied with the question whether socialism would be more successful than capitalism in ensuring rapid technological progress. In a letter written in 1964 he said, 'what is really of prime importance is that of incentives for the growth of productive forces (accumulation and progress in technology). This is the true meaning of, so to say, "rationality" ' (Kowalik 1987b, p. 131). This question, as we shall see, has become a major issue in recent debates.

Lange, as I noted earlier, discussed the 'more refined form' of Mises' argument developed by Hayek and Robbins, which, he claimed, abandoned the essential point made by Mises in so far as the theoretical possibility of a rational allocation of resources in a socialist economy was no longer denied, and only the possibility of a practical solution of the problem was questioned. Thus Hayek ([1935] 1948) in the second of his essays on socialist calculation admitted that it 'is not an impossibility in the sense that it is logically contradictory' to determine, in a socialist society, 'the values and quantities of the different commodities to be produced . . . by the application of the apparatus by which theoretical economics explains the formation of prices and the direction of production in a competitive system' (pp. 152–3). But he then went on to argue that the practical implementation of this procedure would be impossible because of the large mass of data involved. In the first place the collection of these data 'is a task beyond human capacity', and even if this difficulty could be overcome, the next step, of working out the practical decisions, would involve determining hundreds of thousands of 'unknowns' and hence solving this number of equations, 'a task which, with any of the means known at present, could not be carried out in a lifetime' (p. 156). Robbins (1934, p. 151) depicted the problem in still more dramatic terms:

> On paper we can conceive their problem to be solved by a series
> of mathematical calculations. . . . But in practice this solution is

quite unworkable. It would necessitate the drawing up of millions of equations on the basis of millions of statistical data based on many more millions of individual computations. By the time the equations were solved, the information on which they were based would have become obsolete and they would need to be calculated anew.

Lange replied to these arguments in his exposition of the method of trial and error, based on the essay by Taylor; a number of other economists, especially after the experience of wartime planning, also rejected the view that national planning would be a practical impossibility. Thus Devons (1970, p. 97) wrote:

> . . . in the 1930s a great deal of the planning debate in the West was about the system of equations that would need to be solved in a planned economy. . . . Both Western and Russian experience have demonstrated that this theoretical argument is, at present (and, I would argue, as far as we can see ahead in the future) largely irrelevant to the problems of planning in practice.

Schumpeter (1954, pp. 988–9) also rejected the Hayek–Robbins argument that the solutions of the equations required for socialist planning could not be achieved in practice, and took the position of Taylor and Lange that they could be realized by the method of trial and error.

In the third of his essays on socialist calculation Hayek ([1940] 1948) examined critically the mechanism proposed for a socialist economy by Lange, and in a similar form by Dickinson (1939),[6] which he called the 'competitive solution'. After suggesting that 'much of the original claim for the superiority of planning over competition is abandoned if the planned society is now to rely for the direction of its industries to a large extent on competition' (p. 186), he expounded his objections to the method of trial and error as a way of determining the accounting prices of producer goods. First, he argued that, while such a method might work in a world where economic data remained constant over long periods, it would be greatly inferior to market mechanisms in the real world of continual change where reaching the desirable equilibrium depends on the speed with which adjustments can be made (p. 188); he also raised questions about the periods for which the central planning body would fix prices. Second, he deplored the vagueness of both

Lange and Dickinson about the actual organization of the various industries and production units, and went on to pose the question of how the central planners would ensure that their rules concerning the determination of prices were effectively implemented. More generally, he considered some of the problems that might arise in the relations between the 'socialist managers of industry' and the planning authorities (p. 197). Finally, Hayek raised the issue, which became central in his later work, of the preservation of personal and political freedom in a planned economy, expressing the doubt that consumers' choice would be an adequate safeguard against what he called 'arbitrary decisions' taken by those who effectively controlled the economy.

The 'calculation debate' then subsided, partly, as I have suggested, because of the wartime experience of planning, partly because of the revelation during and after the war of the emergence of the Soviet Union as a major industrial power. More recently, however, in the new climate that has developed in some Western capitalist countries, emphasizing individual enterprise and the supremacy of the market, an attempt has been made to revive the debate. Lavoie (1985, p. 4) argues that the protagonists in the original debate did not seem 'to comprehend the fundamental paradigm of their adversaries', so that both sides could claim victory, for or against central planning, and the 'standard accounts' of the debate have perpetuated the confusion. His own aim is to set out more rigorously the theoretical paradigm of the Austrian school, especially Mises and Hayek, and from this standpoint to show that their central arguments against socialist planning have not been refuted. Lavoie focuses on the notion of economic rivalry, and interprets Mises' challenge to socialism 'as an argument for the necessity of a particular kind of rivalry in order to achieve complex social production' (p. 23). After a critical discussion of Marx's socialism, a restatement of Mises' challenge, and an examination of Lange's response in terms of the 'trial and error' method, he goes on to consider the later Austrian rejoinder, and to conclude that Mises had the advantage of the argument in showing that 'the function of this rivalry is to disperse decentralized information' and then marshal it, through market prices, for the purpose of overall economic coordination (p. 180); whereas the ' "trial and error" procedure reduced the choice problem to purely routine behavior, avoiding all the problems of alertness to new opportunities, of futurity, and of knowledge dispersal' (p. 182). Finally, he quotes approvingly Hayek's ([1935] 1948, p. 179) contention that 'nobody has yet demonstrated how planning and competition can be rationally combined' (p. 183).

I shall return in due course to various aspects of Lavoie's thesis, of which I have given a preliminary critical account in a review essay (Bottomore 1986–7), after considering the second major type of criticism of socialist planning: namely, that it is likely to bring about a condition of stagnation through the bureaucratization of economic life, and more widely of social life in general. Max Weber (1918), in his lecture on socialism, was among the first to argue that the changes in modern society indicated an advance towards the 'dictatorship of the official' rather than the 'dictatorship of the proletariat', and 'if private capitalism were eliminated the state bureaucracy would rule *alone*'. Mises (1920) also gave a prominent place to the problems of bureaucracy in his criticism of socialism, and declared indeed that 'it is now universally agreed that the exclusion of free initiative and individual responsibility, on which the successes of private enterprise depend, constitutes the most serious menace to socialist economic organization' (p. 116); while Lange, as we have seen, concluded that 'the real danger of socialism is that of a bureaucratization of economic life'. Schumpeter (1942, p. 206), however, took a very different view

> . . . of that Bureaucratization of Economic Life which constitutes the theme of so many anti-socialist homilies. I for one cannot visualize, in the conditions of modern society, a socialist organization in any form other than that of a huge and all-embracing bureaucratic apparatus. Every other possibility I can conceive would spell failure and breakdown. But surely this should not horrify anyone who realizes how far the bureaucratization of economic life – of life in general even – has gone already. . . . We shall see in the next part that bureaucracy is not an obstacle to democracy but an inevitable complement to it. Similarly it is an inevitable complement to modern economic development and it will be more than ever essential in a socialist commonwealth.

Nevertheless he recognized that bureaucracy gives rise to various problems; in particular its often 'depressing influence on the most active minds', for which there is no simple remedy, and the need for some kind of incentive (beyond 'reliance on a purely altruistic sense of duty') for the efficient performance of functions, which he thought might be provided partly by monetary rewards, but increasingly by the conferment of social prestige.

Many other social scientists, both socialists and their opponents, have contributed to the debate about socialism and bureaucracy – among them Michels (1911), Djilas (1957), Aron (1960, 1965), Hegedüs (1976) – but it has to be said, I think, that much of the discussion has been at least as confused as the 'calculation debate', with the participants adhering firmly to different theoretical conceptions. In order to clarify the issue it is necessary to make a number of distinctions. Bureaucracy may be conceived, in the first place, following Max Weber, as a superior – more rational and efficient – means of administration. In this sense it is one of the principal elements in that process of rationalization of modern societies which was a central theme in Weber's social theory (Löwith 1932, Brubaker 1984). But Weber also conceived bureaucracy, in a narrower sense, as a type of domination, having in mind particularly the role of high state officials in Imperial Germany; and, as we have seen, one of his criticisms of socialism was that it would carry such domination to its extreme limit, where 'the state bureaucracy would rule *alone*'.

In considering the significance of bureaucracy in the socialist countries we have to disentangle these various senses. The general extension of rational administration which is common to all modern societies presents no unique problems in a socialist system, except that the Soviet Union and some other countries had to face initially the difficulties inherited from preceding ramshackle forms of administration; although this was only one part of the much wider problem of creating an educated and efficient labour force at all levels. It was from this aspect of the development of rational administration that Schumpeter expressed his largely favourable view of bureaucratic control of the economy, which I quoted earlier.

The question of bureaucracy as a type of domination raises other issues. Weber thought of it in terms of domination by high officials in the state administration who had usurped, or were usurping, the functions of politicians, and although he was mainly concerned with the somewhat exceptional circumstances of Imperial Germany, the degree of independent power and influence wielded by the 'administrative élite' has been widely discussed in other contexts (Bottomore 1964). But the type of domination – autocratic or totalitarian – which developed in the Soviet Union, and after 1945 in the other socialist countries of Eastern Europe, was domination by a *party* whose leaders concentrated all political power in their own hands, and in due course in the hands of a single individual, rather than by an administrative élite. As this kind of regime became established, however, and after the savagery of Stalin's rule had ended, there emerged a system characterized by the dominance of party and state officials who constituted, in the view of some critics, a 'new class' (Djilas 1957, Konrád and Szelényi 1979). The evolution of the communist parties in the socialist countries exemplifies indeed the process which Weber termed the 'routinization of charisma', as well as the oligarchical tendencies described by Michels, and it was this process, along with the vast expansion of bureaucratic administration to implement central planning, in societies where public criticism and any kind of opposition were rigorously suppressed, which produced the stagnation, inefficiency and corruption that have become the principal targets of current policies of economic and political reform.

In the 1940s and throughout the post-war period, the critique of socialist planning came to concentrate much more upon the lack of freedom and the totalitarian regulation of all aspects of social life than upon the difficulties of economic calculation, and many socialists, as well as their opponents, elaborated fundamental criticisms of the Soviet model of a planned society. Thus Hilferding (1940, 1941) argued that the Soviet Union was a 'totalitarian state economy' and pointed to the dangers resulting from the great increase in the power of the modern state and the extension of its activities into all spheres of life, which led to 'the subjection of the economy by the holders of state power'. This theme of the merging of economic and political power, and its concentration in the activities of the state, became pre-eminent in the later discussions, and most influential in the writings of conservative critics.

Hayek ([1940] 1948) in the course of discussing Dickinson's (1939) book raised, as I noted, the question of personal freedom in a centrally planned society. In addition to making frequent references to what he always describes as the 'arbitrary' decisions of the economic planners – though why these should be considered arbitrary, or more arbitrary than the decisions made by many governments in other types of society, is never made clear or even examined – he went on to criticize particularly Dickinson's statement that 'in a socialist society the distinction, always artificial, between economics and politics will break down; the economic and the political machinery of society will fuse into one', concluding that 'this is, of course, precisely the authoritarian doctrine preached by Nazis and Fascists' (p. 207). Later, in what became a very influential tract, *The Road to Serfdom* (1944), Hayek expressed his opposition to socialism and central planning in still stronger terms, and he has continued, up to his most recent work (1982), to advocate a 'spontaneous' or 'self-generating' order of society in which the powers of government would be strictly delimited and confined.

Aron, in a similar though more restrained fashion, analysed the Soviet Union as a totalitarian regime in which a single party has a monopoly of political activity, an official state ideology is imposed by coercion and persuasion, and most economic and professional activities are subject to the state, or even, in a way, part of it ([1965] 1988, ch. 15); and in several essays (notably [1950] 1988, ch. 6) he contrasted the 'unified élite' in the Soviet Union with the plurality of rival élites in the capitalist democracies.

In the post-war years, therefore, a broad agreement seemed to emerge among social scientists about the nature of the political regime in the Soviet Union and in the countries of Eastern Europe (excluding Yugoslavia), although there were many different nuances in the critical assessments, and these became more pronounced as the Stalinist era receded. But there was much disagreement about the relation between central planning, or the socialist project as a whole, and political dictatorship. Some, like Hayek, argued that central planning and the merging of the economic and political spheres necessarily led to an authoritarian political system and the loss of personal freedom. Others, however, saw the Soviet dictatorship as the outcome, rather, of the absence of democratic traditions and experience – instead of which there persisted a tradition of authoritarian rule (and the idea of the 'good tsar'); of the forced industrialization of the 1930s inspired in part by the fear of capitalist encirclement and the danger of military intervention; of the Cold War in the post-war period which revived earlier fears; and perhaps, more generally, of the tendency of all revolutions (as well as counter-revolutions) to institute, for longer or shorter periods, highly authoritarian regimes. From this perspective it was possible to envisage a gradual democratization of Soviet society and of the East European societies, in the long term; a process which evidently began after the death of Stalin and has accelerated notably in recent years.

The main concern of this book is the organization and functioning of socialist economies, though I shall return later to an examination of the relations between the economic and political regimes; and in the economic sphere I think it is possible, at this juncture, in the light of the criticisms so far considered, to construct a preliminary balance sheet of the achievements and failures of socialist planning. In the first place, it can be said that the main objections brought forward in the calculation debate greatly exaggerated the difficulties, whether theoretical or practical, of planning; and they seem to have even less validity in the age of super-computers. Nevertheless, two issues arising from that debate are still important. One relates to the complexity, especially in terms of the immense variety of goods and services supplied, of modern production; in this context many critics have argued that while central planning may be effective where there is a single clearly defined aim to be achieved – for example, rapid industrialization or the construction of a war economy, accompanied in both cases by severe constraints on individual consumption, choice of occupation, and so on, which are more or less willingly accepted by, or imposed upon, the population in order to attain the goal – it is less effective in developing the production and distribution of the great range of consumer goods and services characteristic of a modern society.

Such criticism is also relevant to two other matters. First, it is clear that central planning and the organization of large-scale production have been generally far less successful in agriculture than in industry, and that an effective agricultural policy in many of the socialist countries has still to be worked out. This relative failure is connected, in part, with the very high rates of investment in industry which have continued up to the present time; but it also requires, and is now receiving, a thorough reassessment of the kind of economic regime most appropriate to agricultural production (which would include individual cultivation and small partnerships or cooperatives, as well as state farms) and to the distribution of the product. Second, the quality as well as the quantity and variety of goods and services in many of the socialist countries is notoriously unsatisfactory, and this is connected partly with the absence from the central planning mechanism of adequate quality inspection (except, as is generally recognized, in the privileged spheres of the space programme and military production), partly with failures of management, and partly, as free-market critics would insist, with the lack of alternative sources of supply and of some degree of competition between producers. These critical reflections raise a host of questions about management and incentives, about bureaucratic regulation, and about the place of market mechanisms in a socialist economy, which will be examined in some detail in the following two chapters. There is a second issue, however, related to all of these, and quite central to the revived calculation debate, which should be considered at this point; namely, the capacity for innovation in socialist economies. Lavoie (1985), as I noted earlier, has claimed that the later socialist arguments against Mises and Hayek ignored 'all the problems of alertness to new opportunities, of futurity, and of knowledge dispersal' which are 'crucial to any analysis of choice in the real world' (p. 182), and a number of other writers have emphasized the importance of this problem in the Soviet economy. Berliner (1988), for example, in essays written in the 1970s, discusses the question of 'bureaucratic creativity', particularly of the 'planning bureaucracy', with respect to technological innovation, and while recognizing that 'the system has been effective in generating an enormous volume of new technology' (p. 201),[7] observes that there are many factors inhibiting innovation, above all the conservatism of the planning bureaucracy and an aversion to excessive risk-taking, so that new technology is less rapidly and less comprehensively introduced than would be desirable. In a later essay (pp. 246–66) he considers the prospects for technological progress in the context of the sharp decline in the rate of economic growth which became apparent in the 1970s, and notes the conclusion of most Western research that in the post-war period technological progress in the Soviet Union was considerably less rapid than in the advanced capitalist countries, where technological advances became a much more important source of growth than increases in labour and capital inputs (p. 249).

The Soviet economic system of centralized planning, which Berliner describes as 'a reasonably successful structure' that attained in the first thirty-five years of planning 'an impressive rate of economic and industrial growth' (p. 246), seems no longer entirely appropriate to the new conditions and the recognition of this situation underlies the present drive for economic 'restructuring' in the Soviet Union and other socialist countries, which was foreshadowed by the 'Prague Spring' of 1968 (see especially the discussion of a transition from extensive to intensive growth, and of the role of knowledge in production, in Richta 1969) and by the Hungarian 'New Economic Mechanism' introduced in that same year.[8]

Overall, it may be concluded, central planning has been successful in most of the European socialist countries in achieving fast and stable economic growth (Buck and Cole 1987, ch. 8) and transforming them into major industrial producers who now account for about one-third of the world's industrial output, but it has not yet raised per capita income and living standards, except in one or two cases, to the level of the advanced capitalist countries, and since the 1970s the rate of growth has declined (though this has also happened in most of the capitalist countries, and it is a widely held view that economic growth is likely to be slower in mature economies). Most important, perhaps, is the fact that the introduction of new technology seems to be more sluggish in the Soviet Union and other socialist countries than in many capitalist countries, but this may be explained in part at least by the more recent 'maturation' of the socialist economies and in consequence a later recognition of the need to move towards intensive, technology-based, growth.

Two other considerations should be borne in mind in assessing the results of socialist planing thus far. First, as has occasionally been noted, the economic achievements of the Soviet Union and some other socialist countries would have appeared still more impressive if the development of capitalist economies after the Second World War had reproduced the conditions of the inter-war years, instead of entering upon a period of unprecedentedly rapid growth. The post-war successes of capitalism, in spite of considerable fluctuations which have become more frequent in the 1980s, are therefore a major element in the comparison between capitalist and socialist economies, and they deserve some more systematic explanation than has yet, to my knowledge, been attempted. Here, without pretending even to sketch any kind of general explanation – which would require a study on the scale of Schumpeter's (1939) work on business cycles – I would simply observe that these successes have occurred alongside massive increases in state intervention and expenditure and a considerable extension of national economic planning in a variety of forms; and that a broad view of post-war development suggests that the advanced capitalist countries which have had more comprehensive national planning, and in some cases more extensive public ownership of industry, have been more successful than others (two good examples being the contrast in economic performance between Japan and the United States and between France and Britain). In the long term, as I shall argue in more detail later, not only does a fairly high level of economic planning seem likely to be advantageous everywhere, but socialist economies, in a context of reformed political and economic institutions, offer greater hope for sustained and stable growth, in addition to their other advantages (such as Lange emphasized) in the kind of distribution of wealth and income that they establish, and more generally in what may be summarily described as their pursuit of 'the greatest good of the greatest number'.

However, a second point that we have to consider is the nature and consequences of innovation and growth. Many people in the capitalist countries (and, for that matter, increasingly in some socialist countries) have become uncomfortably aware that technological progress is not an unmixed blessing, and share the doubts expressed by Gabor (1970) about 'compulsive innovation' and 'growth addiction'.[9] From this aspect, the slower rate of innovation in socialist societies, if such is the case, may not be altogether a disadvantage. But this is not the main issue. The question is rather: what kinds of new technology and economic growth are likely to add most to the sum of human happiness and to the quality of life? This question can only find a partial resolution – and always, I would think, in a tentative and corrigible way – within a clearly defined social policy. Thus, in present-day Britain, it would be advantageous, and to judge by opinion polls is seen by a majority of the population to be advantageous, to transfer resources from the increase of purely private wealth to the improvement of the national health service and education, the protection of the environment, and a general expansion of public amenities; and the recent emphasis by the EC on a 'social Europe' suggests that such a view is becoming more widespread. In principle, a socialist society is better equipped, through the machinery of central planning and in terms of its basic doctrine, to move along such a path; and now that the phase of rapid industrialization and growth has been completed in many of the European socialist societies, it should be expected that they will develop in a more discriminating fashion with regard to both innovation and growth, and with the advantage of having already a solid infrastructure of publicly provided services.

Nevertheless, in spite of the undoubted achievements and potentialities of the developed socialist economies, there is a fairly general recognition that they are now facing serious problems, which are increasingly seen to arise, not so much from difficulties of economic calculation, as from bureaucratic rigidities and conservatism, inadequate incentives for efficient production, the excessive centralization of power and decision-making, and a corresponding frustration of the exercise of initiative, choice and critical judgement by individuals and associations whose actions and relationships constitute the tissue of social life. It is these problems and the reforming policies which are being implemented, or are proposed, in order to deal with them which have to be examined more closely in the following chapters.

Notes

1. Wieser was a moderate critic of socialism and, indeed, quite sympathetic to social democratic ideas (Hutchison 1981, p. 207); Böhm-Bawerk a much more committed opponent; and Mises the most vehement critic of all.
2. See also Schumpeter (1954, pp. 986–7).
3. Böhm-Bawerk's and Hilferding's texts are published together in a volume edited with an introduction by Paul Sweezy (1949).
4. Lange (p. 60) cites Wicksteed (1933) to the effect that price in the narrower sense of the money for which a good or service can be obtained is simply a special case of price in the wider sense, and he notes that Schumpeter (1908) similarly used the term 'exchange ratio' in this wider sense.
5. To simplify the problem Lange assumed that all means of production are publicly owned, but noted that 'in any actual socialist community there must be a large number of means of production privately owned (e.g. by farmers, artisans, and small-scale entrepreneurs)' (p. 73).

6. Dickinson's work, praised by Hayek as 'a book of great distinction', provides a very clear account of how a socialist economy might be organized, with a combination of consumer choice and central planning, reviewing different options and various objections. In most respects it is close to the model proposed by Taylor and Lange, though it seems to restrict more stringently the sphere of private enterprise.

7. In connection with Soviet technological achievement, which is often denigrated by the more extreme Western critics, it is important to draw attention to areas of conspicuous success, for example, in the space programme, but also in the work of various institutes of technology. The Paton Institute in Kiev, for example, is well known as a centre of high technology which revolutionized tank construction during the Second World War by the development of automated welding techniques (making possible the mass production of the outstanding Soviet T-34 tank) and has continued to innovate in industrial technology which is used by many Western countries, including Britain (for example, for the pipelines which bring North Sea oil ashore).

8. The social ideas and movements of the late 1960s were among the most encouraging and innovative of the post-war era, and, after their decline or suppression, world politics entered a sordid and depressing phase from which they are only now beginning to emerge, largely as a result of the transformations taking place in the socialist countries.

9. See my discussion of some of these issues in Bottomore (1975, ch. 12).

5

The state, bureaucracy and self-management

The economic role of the state has been greatly extended in all modern societies, and most of all in the socialist planned societies, where the process gave rise to all the familiar, and quite justified, criticisms of totalitarianism and dictatorship. But there is not a necessary connection between the expansion of the state's economic activities and the emergence of political dictatorship or authoritarian rule. Everything depends upon the nature of the political system. In the Soviet Union and Eastern Europe it was the monopoly of political power by a single party, in the context of other factors which I discussed earlier, that produced totalitarian, and subsequently authoritarian, regimes of greater or lesser harshness. What may plausibly be argued is that centralized control of the economy, and in some degree a merging of the economic and political systems, creates conditions in which a 'unified élite', or a new dominant class, can more easily emerge. But this is not bound to happen; nor, on the other hand, is it the case that societies in which private enterprise prevails and there is little central planning invariably escape such conditions. There are, and have been, plenty of examples of political dictatorship and authoritarian rule in such societies.

The question of government in a socialist society has to be tackled directly by considering what political institutions this kind of society, in which the major productive resources are public property and the class relations of capitalist society no longer exist, might have. Debate on this subject was for many decades hampered or excluded by the prevalence of a particular interpretation of Marxist thought, according to which there could be no fundamental disagreements on matters of social and economic policy in a society where the working class – represented by *its* party, or in due course by the party leaders – was in power, and where the eventual 'withering away' of all political power could be envisaged, even though the repressive power of the state was, in fact, being continually increased. This doctrine, though hardly the practice, could find some support in Marx's own ideas, the Utopian element in which is not far removed from William Morris's vision of a society whose affairs are conducted entirely by voluntary and spontaneous cooperation. But the harsh experience of political despotism and terror, and more recently the slowing down of economic growth, have produced a gradual modification of the doctrine (in conditions, both internal and external, which differ radically from those of the period from the 1920s to the 1950s), which now shows a greater affinity with the more pragmatic views often expressed by Marx and Engels themselves, as well as by some later Marxists, to the effect that the precise characteristics and institutions of a socialist society could not be fully defined in advance, and there would be much learning to be done 'after the revolution'.

It remains the case, however, that many Marxist and other socialist thinkers, belonging to diverse schools, took for granted that an organized working-class party would rule the new society, more or less unchallenged, at least during a period of transition which might be quite prolonged, and their ideas were remote from those now being expressed in the discussions about 'political pluralism'. Such pluralism – that is to say, electoral competition between candidates representing different groups or parties, and greater freedom for the activities of various social movements – the first steps towards which are being taken in some of the socialist countries, and most boldly in Poland and Hungary, is intended to extend public debate and choice in the sphere of economic and social policy, and to diminish further the scope of authoritarian rule; and it is evidently conceived not simply as a process of 'democratization' but as an essential element in the reform and reinvigoration of the economy.

Before turning to that central issue of this book, it is important to consider some of the wider implications of political pluralism. No one can be sure in advance how the current changes will evolve, or what policies will emerge from the new structure of politics. It is possible, though perhaps not very likely in the foreseeable future in most of the socialist countries, that competition for political leadership on an extensive scale will lead to the emergence of influential pro-capitalist forces tending towards a restoration, or partial restoration of capitalism. The possibility of such an outcome clearly poses fundamental questions about socialist, and more specifically Marxist, conceptions of social development, in which the attainment of socialism is seen as being, in a stronger or weaker sense, a determined and irreversible stage in a progressive movement of history. Certainly there was no place in Marx's theory for the idea of a reverse transition from socialism to capitalism, or to some third, unimagined form of society. Yet the future development of the advanced industrial societies does now appear more open, less determined and predictable, than many socialist thinkers have been inclined to recognize, and there is correspondingly an urgent need to re-examine, in a fundamental way, our conceptions of the political forms of socialism.

Such an exercise is beyond the scope of this book, but there are still some other aspects of the relation between state power and central planning that need to be considered. The idea of political pluralism should not be confined, as it often seems to be, to the subject of free elections and competing parties. Just as important is the decentralization of political power by enhancing the role of local and regional government within nation states (and this is relevant also in the case of some capitalist countries, notably in Britain, where the powers of local government have been steadily reduced by an increasingly authoritarian central government), and the working out of electoral systems which allow the widest possible representation of diverse interests and of preferences in social policy. It was never reasonable to suppose that in a socialist society all conflicts of interest or diversity of aims would disappear, even after the abolition of major class differences (which, for that matter, may reappear in new forms), and it may well be the case in the future that political power in socialist societies will not only be more decentralized, but will frequently be exercised by coalition governments which change their complexion and orientation from time to time as circumstances change.

But there is still another element of vital importance in a pluralistic system; namely, the development of a great variety of active associations in civil society. Such associations – occupational, economic, community-based, environmental, or cultural – while being independent of the state, may have a significant influence on social policy as primary sources of the individual's capacity to choose, innovate and participate in making decisions on matters directly affecting the quality of his or her life. The ideas of 'participatory democracy' and 'self-management' both express the immense importance of this dense network of non-state associations as the substratum and condition of effective democratic pluralism.

Finally, however, we should not be led into assuming that the nation state, even when it is deeply involved in centralized economic planning, is the only serious threat to individual liberty (or as it would be preferable to say, to the specific and particular liberties of individuals and social groups). It is well to bear in mind here, in considering the political institutions of socialist society in relation to its economic organization, the discussion of the state, democracy and citizenship by that exemplary liberal sociologist L. T. Hobhouse, who sagely remarked that 'there are other enemies of liberty besides the State, and it is in fact by the State that we have fought them' (Hobhouse 1922, p.83).

The aspect of the state in a planned socialist society that has attracted most attention and criticism ever since Max Weber wrote of the 'dictatorship of the official' is the growth of bureaucracy and its consequences. This has both a political and an economic dimension, and in the following discussion I shall concentrate on the latter, since, as I have already argued, the question of political power and the emergence of a new dominant class or élite in socialist societies requires an analysis of the nature of the state, and of the monopolization of power by a single party, rather than of bureaucracy in its most general sense. To be sure, there has also grown up a party bureaucracy which has a significant role in the economy, and its influence will be considered in the relevant contexts, but I shall begin by examining the bureaucratic phenomenon as it manifests itself in the planning and regulation of economic life by state officials and managers.

A useful starting point is to be found in the discussion by Berliner (1988, ch. 8), who distinguishes two levels of bureaucracy in the

Soviet system: a 'planning bureaucracy' which is 'interposed between the firms and the Party leadership' and comprises the economic ministries, organizations dealing with the planning process and finance, and segments of the Party bureaucracy; and the management bureaucracy in individual firms, which is comparable with that in capitalist corporations and hence referred to as the 'corporate bureaucracy'. Berliner then goes on to consider the conservatism or creativity of these two bureaucracies, in relation to the problem of motivation, and notes that they tend to make 'those decisions which contribute to a higher score on the standards by which their own work is evaluated. In some cases, this leads to creative behaviour; in others to conservative behaviour. The crux of the issue is the standard of evaluation.' (p.193) But there is also a general obstacle to creativity: namely, the lack of satisfactory quantitative indicators of the relative value of commodities as implied by the preferences of the party leadership, since the 'shadow prices' which express the relative values are not in fact known by the central planners, the planning bureaucracy, or the firms (p.195).

The outcome is that the whole bureaucratic system tends to be conservative rather than creative, and although the system 'has been effective in generating an enormous volume of new technology' this is not the same as efficiency, which 'refers to the relationship between the magnitude of the results and the magnitude of the effort and resources invested' (p. 201). In general, there is little doubt that the rate of technological innovation and of productivity growth (which reflects greater efficiency) has been unsatisfactory,[1] and since the 1960s a succession of major reforms and minor changes have been introduced, revised, and sometimes reversed again, in an effort to improve efficiency and increase the rate of economic growth (Berliner 1988, ch. 12). What has changed most fundamentally is the conception of central planning. Whereas the Stalinist leadership, as Berliner (*ibid.*, p. 280) remarks, had great faith in the ability of the central planners, who had after all achieved the transformation of the Soviet Union into a great industrial power, to direct the economy in every detail, 'that naive optimism has long since vanished' and the aim of all the subsequent reforms has been to find a way of decentralizing local decisions in the framework of a central plan.

So far, however, the internal structure of firms has changed relatively little in the Soviet Union, although the organizational structure above the level of the firm has undergone considerable changes, so that, as Berliner (*ibid.*, p. 275) observes, 'the bureaucracy that stands between enterprise director and his minister is much more complex than in the pre-war period'. Elsewhere, notably in Yugoslavia from the 1950s and in Hungary since 1968, there have been more fundamental changes in enterprise structure, as well as in the economic system generally, with the development of diverse forms of 'market socialism'; and the current policy of restructuring the economy in the Soviet Union points in the same direction. The aim is to create new opportunities and incentives for efficient management, leading to more rapid technological innovation and higher productivity, less wasteful use of resources, and the elimination of all kinds of bottlenecks in the supply of materials to productive enterprises and in the distribution of consumer goods, both by liberating enterprises from detailed central regulation and by introducing an element of competition.

One consequence of deregulation and the greater autonomy of enterprises is quite clearly a reduction in the size of the bureaucracy, which itself represents a considerable saving of resources. Nuti (1988) notes 'the drastic personnel reduction of the Central Planning Commission' (p. 377) in the Soviet Union, and also the substantial reduction in the number of ministries responsible for industrial sectors, which in Hungary and Poland have been replaced by a single Ministry for Industry and Trade (p. 378). The achievement of smaller, more efficient bureaucracies responsible for the general management of the economy, by dismantling central planning in the form of detailed physical control of enterprises and sectors, would be a considerable gain, both economically and politically, for many of the socialist countries; but the question of the nature of central planning and its relation to markets in the new economic system is far from being resolved, and, as Nuti (*ibid.*, p. 382) suggests, the success of the restructuring process may mean that 'the traditional problems of centrally planned economies will have been alleviated or perhaps solved, but at the cost of introducing at least some of the problems of capitalist economies'.

This difficult issue will be examined in the next chapter; meanwhile it is necessary to look at the diverse structures of individual enterprises and the changes they are undergoing in the socialist countries, in relation to bureaucracy and to economic performance. The first major break with the Stalinist system took place in

Yugoslavia, with the introduction of a new economic and social policy based upon the self-management of enterprises and other social and cultural institutions. The Yugoslav economy can be characterized briefly by saying that property is managed directly by the workers themselves, in a system of social ownership which is contrasted with state ownership in other socialist countries.[2] The latter separates the means of production from the producers in a new way and creates new dominant groups of party officials, bureaucrats and managers; whereas social ownership approaches more closely the conception of a 'society of associated producers', formulated abstractly by Marx, but influenced by the experience of cooperative factories in the nineteenth century.

In a system of state ownership, the coordination of the economy as a whole is assured by some central authority – the central planners and the party leadership – as has been the case in the Soviet Union and other socialist countries until quite recently; but where enterprises are in principle autonomous and self-managed, the relations between them have to be established in a different way, namely through the market and exchange, though in an economy which is still planned and subject to a general regulation by the state. The economic advantages of this system were seen as being that the producers are no longer directly subordinated to external political authorities, that incomes are determined by output and productivity instead of by administrative decisions, and that the independence of the producers provides greater incentives for economic development. But the restructuring of the Yugoslav economy also had the wider aim of encouraging the full participation of citizens in determining their social life and achieving responsible self-government in a genuine socialist democracy.

The initial achievements of Yugoslavia under the new regime were impressive, with very high growth rates and a high level of accumulation and investment, and they attracted widespread attention. But unemployment remained high, resulting in large-scale emigration of labour, mainly to West Germany, and economic disparities between regions tended to grow, as did income differences generally. More recently, economic performance has greatly deteriorated, the country is burdened with massive external debt, and the economic failures along with the continuing disparities between regions have exacerbated cultural and political tensions within this multinational state. As a result, criticisms of the existing self-management system, which were already voiced in the late 1960s, have multiplied both inside and outside Yugoslavia.[3]

The major problems of self-management seem to be the following. First, economic efficiency varies considerably, for diverse reasons, between enterprises, and this results in significant differences in income and social benefits between the workers in these enterprises. It also raises the question of whether the least efficient enterprises should be allowed to go bankrupt and, in that case, what becomes of their employees and of socialist policies of full and stable employment. Beyond this, according to some critics, there has developed in the more successful enterprises a 'group-egoism', and the property relations that have been established could more accurately be described as 'group ownership' rather than 'social ownership'.

Second, the full participation of employees in self-management is rarely achieved. Just as in self-managed associations of various types in other societies (for example, voluntary associations created for charitable and educational purposes), most members are passive supporters, whereas there is always an active minority of individuals who are ready, or eager, to take on administrative tasks and exercise some authority. In Yugoslavia the level of participation in management varies considerably between enterprises and regions, and in the most favourable cases may attain some 40 per cent of the work force; but it is generally much lower than this, and in the view of some critics an 'oligarchy' or 'meritocracy' has developed both within enterprises and in the political/administrative system. Nevertheless, it may be argued that the Yugoslav system has demonstrated its feasibility over a fairly long period, and as Széll (1988, p.113) observes, 'it has proved that simple workers are able, without being experts, to run companies and social institutions, and that this society therefore provides some hope that political apathy will be overcome'.

Third, in an economy in which the basic productive units are independent self-managed enterprises, the coordination of economic activity as a whole is effected partly by market relations, partly by central and regional planning, giving rise to a major problem concerning the relationship between the autonomous activity of production collectives and rational economic planning (Supek, cited by Széll 1988, p. 108). This is the main subject of the following chapter, and here it will be enough to place the question in the broader context of an assessment of the achievements and difficulties of the Yugoslav project. The intention of the structural changes in the Yugoslav economy and society, which have been steadily developed over a period of almost forty years now, was, as I have said, to approach more closely the condition of a mature socialist society, conceived as a 'society of associated producers'. Undoubtedly, the changes have brought substantial achievements. Throughout this period, until the very recent wave of liberalization in much of Eastern Europe, Yugoslavia has been a far more open society than any of the other socialist countries, and in the 1960s especially, the future prospect looked exceptionally bright, above all in so far as economic development was concerned. The extent of these achievements can be judged from one aspect by the fact that the Yugoslav system became to some extent a model, though not to be followed in every detail, for other socialist countries in Eastern Europe and also for China, when they embarked upon a major restructuring of their economies.

A principal feature of the new Yugoslav economy was what came to be called 'market socialism', though a better term might be 'socialism with markets', as has been suggested by Tomlinson (in Hindess 1989), and this has become a fashionable phrase in recent studies and debates. In the Yugoslav case, however, it was only a part of the overall project to create a socialist society, the main pillar of which was to be the self-management of enterprises and institutions as a way of involving the whole population in the determination of economic and social policy and countering the growth of new élites. But these two elements were inseparably connected, for the autonomy of enterprises necessitated the development of market relations among them, within a framework of regulation which included national economic planning, the protection of consumer interests, and the provision of general infrastructural and welfare services. Moreover, market relations and competition among independent producers were seen as valuable in themselves in so far as they promoted greater economic efficiency and higher growth rates.

What is evident from the Yugoslav experience, however, is that the attainment of socialism as a 'society of associated producers' is an infinitely more difficult process than was ever imagined by earlier socialist thinkers, or by those who subsequently endeavoured to achieve it in the wake of social revolutions. On one side, central planning implemented by a single party which claims a monopoly of power as the maker of the revolution facilitates the growth of a new dominant and privileged group in society, and the planning itself may be less effective once the initial phase of rapid industrialization has been completed, and the planners themselves become increasingly concerned with the promotion of their own sectional interests. On the other side, as has been seen in considering the Yugoslav system, self-management may also give rise to new sectional interests, of the enterprises themselves, and result in growing inequalities of income and difficulties in coordinating economic development as a whole.

A major study of the problems in Yugoslavia by Horvat (1982) proposes personal taxation as a means of reducing income disparities (as has now been undertaken in Hungary), the exclusion of culture, education and health from the market, and a restructuring of the functions of government. There is also now an animated debate throughout Eastern Europe on the establishment of a multi-party system, already partially implemented in Hungary and Poland, or at the least a system in which various groups, not formally constituted as parties, can contest elections and express public criticism of economic and social policies; and development along these lines seems quite likely in Yugoslavia and the Soviet Union itself. These political changes, which are very widely recognized as being a crucial element in the process of economic restructuring and renewal, will be discussed further in later chapters, but we have yet to consider another vital aspect of the economic problems and changes in the socialist countries.

Markets, *pace* the champions of *laissez-faire*, are not a universal panacea for economic ills, as the citizens of capitalist countries have long known and as those in some socialist countries have been rediscovering; and they certainly do not offer a royal road to socialism. Competition and markets may bring benefits to consumers, increase the efficiency of producers, and stimulate economic growth (though this is not always, as the case of Britain shows, the kind of growth which is sustainable or most beneficial in the medium or long term); but at the same time they are likely to bring greater instability and economic inequality, and perhaps a deterioration of collective provision and the sense of community. In a socialist society these problems, as I have indicated in discussing the Yugoslav system of self-management and markets, are considerable, and have become the subject of intense debate, and they are compounded by a further element which deserves particular attention. With the development of markets and the greater independence of enterprises, many socialist countries have become increasingly involved in the capitalist world market and hence exposed to the economic cycles characteristic of capitalism. With the recession in the capitalist countries in the 1980s, some of the East European socialist countries have faced major problems of adverse foreign trade balances and large external debts, the latter resulting from ill-advised large-scale borrowing at a time when Western banks were only too ready to lend their massive cash resources all over the world. At the present time, Poland, Hungary and Yugoslavia are particularly affected by these conditions, and we shall need to consider later how far the most recent policies of economic reform, and especially those in the Soviet Union, will be able to avoid this kind of dependence. The underlying factor is undoubtedly the continuing relative weakness of the socialist economies, despite their considerable achievements. No socialist country or group of countries has yet become economically powerful enough to have a determining influence on the world economy, and although there is not, in my view, a single world system, as some have argued, there is certainly a still dominant capitalist system, confronted by an alternative socialist system, which is economically weaker and as yet incapable of exerting so powerful an influence.

In later chapters I shall consider how far the present economic reforms in socialist countries are likely to change this situation, which is similar, on a world scale, to that which has been noted in respect of the attempts to move towards socialism in the capitalist world itself, where a single country, or even a small group of countries, seems generally doomed to failure in a confrontation with the power of international capitalism sustained mainly, at least until recently, by the United States.[4] Clearly, the conditions would be greatly changed by a revival of the socialist economies in Eastern Europe, and there are already signs that the new policies there are beginning to have an effect, with an increase in the rate of economic growth to 4 per cent in 1988 and a significant rise in foreign trade.[5] But a rapid and sustained improvement in economic performance depends crucially upon how successfully the restructuring of these economies is carried out, and the central issue, to which I shall now turn, is unquestionably that of creating a system which successfully combines central (plus regional and local) planning with markets in a socialist economy.

Notes

1. See also the comments by Nuti (1988, pp. 373–4): 'Research and development have tended to be academically oriented and detached from the needs of both industry and teaching; the innovation decision has remained by and large an administrative decision; long investment gestation has led to intolerable delays in the introduction of new techniques. What is worse, several reasons appear to provide a positive disincentive for enterprise managers to innovate.' Nuti goes on to list some of the major disincentives and concludes: 'It is not surprising, therefore, that R & D and productivity trends have been quite disappointing outside a few sectors such as space and military industries.'
2. For more detailed accounts of the Yugoslav system see Broekmeyer (1970) and Széll (1988, pp. 104–11).
3. See, for example, Stojanović (1973) and Széll (1988, pp. 112–23).
4. See the discussion in Holland (1983) of the need to restructure the West European economies in a joint effort by the EC countries.
5. United Nations Economic Commission for Europe, *Economic Survey of Europe in 1988-9*.

6

Plan and market

Ever since the debates about central planning and socialist calculation in the 1930s, and more particularly since the formulation by Lange and Dickinson of what Hayek called the 'competitive solution', according to which prices and the allocation of productive resources were to be determined by a combination of market mechanisms and central planning, there has been continued discussion of the ways in which planning and markets can be successfully integrated in a socialist society. The discussion has been especially intense in Yugoslavia, where critics have singled out as a major problem the relation between self-managed enterprises operating in a market situation and the requirements of rational economic planning (see above, p.77); and in recent years, with the new wave of economic reforms, it has spread widely throughout Eastern Europe. But the general question is one of great complexity, which has many different aspects, and we should begin by distinguishing some of the separate issues involved.

First, there is a great difference between those societies in which the greater part of productive resources are publicly owned and central planning has a major role in the economy, and on the other hand, the societies in which there is only limited public ownership and planning and the construction of a socialist economy involves some extension of planning in diverse forms, along with restrictions on market mechanisms. In this chapter I shall be concerned with the former group of countries, and primarily with the East European socialist societies, deferring until a later chapter a discussion of the second group, mainly in Western Europe, where at various times – and in some cases over fairly long periods, as for example in Sweden – the countries concerned have moved towards a more socialist form of society. But within the group of existing socialist countries itself there are important differences, arising from distinctive economic, social and cultural conditions, which are revealed in the very different course of post-war development in, for example, the Soviet Union, Yugoslavia, Hungary, the German Democratic Republic and Poland. So it is not to be expected that precisely the same solutions will be tried in every country, although there will certainly be some common policies and a continuation of the exchange of ideas and experiences such as has already been taking place; hence it will be necessary to look also at the specific problems and reforms in particular countries.

Second, the restructuring of the socialist economies raises questions not only about the scope and nature of central planning, but also about the forms of ownership of productive resources, and in particular the extent to which private ownership will be permitted or encouraged. This is not a new issue in socialist debate, and very diverse views have been expounded about the ownership of property in a socialist society. A clear distinction was always made between personal property – which would only be affected by the transition to socialism to the extent that a greater equality between individuals became established – and ownership of productive resources; the divergences of view concerned essentially the latter kind of property, above all in the basic spheres of economic activity and where ownership was highly concentrated in the hands of small groups of people through the development of large corporations in industry and finance. Marx's legacy – the conception of the 'associated producers' – seemed to imply a very wide extension of social ownership, and a virtual extinction of individual ownership, but, as we saw in the case of Kautsky, those early Marxists who gave any attention to the practical organization of a socialist economy were quite ready to envisage very diverse forms of ownership, including a sphere of individual ownership and private production. Furthermore, there was from the beginning, among Marxists and other socialists, a powerful current of thought which favoured relatively independent self-managed enterprises, while opposing centrally planned and managed state industries; and such ideas not only persisted but enjoyed frequent revivals, as in the councils movement and in the Yugoslav system.[1] From this protracted debate and accumulated practical experience it is evident that the structure of a socialist economy still remains an 'unsettled question', to which different answers may be given in different countries and in changing historical circumstances.

Third, the debate about property ownership is intimately connected, as I have indicated, with the question of central planning and state industries. Many socialists, and writers on socialism, have recognized that a socialist economy cannot simply be equated with central planning. Hayek ([1935] 1948, p.130), for example, distinguished between 'socialism' as a description of ends and 'planning' as a method, and argued that 'it is possible to have much planning with little socialism or little planning and much socialism'. In the writings of some of the Utopian socialists it was assumed or hoped, as in the case of Morris, that a spontaneous order would emerge from the activities of responsible, cooperative individuals, without any elaborate machinery of government, administration or economic management, though other Utopians, like Bellamy, envisaged a powerful central authority which would regulate social life. The supporters of workers' councils and self-management, in a less extreme way, advocated the autonomy of productive enterprises on the basis of social ownership, but they did not consider in detail how the diverse economic activities would be coordinated, and, as we have seen, the self-management system implies the existence of markets and, in practice, creates difficult problems of the kind that I discussed earlier, in particular the specific problem of a symbiosis between plan and market.

At all events, in the mainstream of socialist thought and practice the concept of planning came to be closely identified with socialism, and as Dickinson (1939, p. 9) wrote:

> The definition of socialism that was generally accepted during the half-century between 1875 and 1925 is 'social ownership of the means of production'. Since that time the phrase 'planned production' has been tending to take its place. There is a close connexion between these two definitions. . . . One fundamental difference between socialism and capitalism will be the existence of an authority able to view the economic system as a whole and with power

to make decisions involving the system as a whole.

Another half-century later the question of planning has become much more complicated and the subject of renewed controversy. On one side, the continued development of 'organized capitalism'[2] has enlarged the sphere of planning and the role of the state in capitalist economies, particularly in the most dynamic societies, such as Japan. On the other side, comprehensive central planning in the socialist countries seems to have run into serious difficulties, and to be less effective in a more complex advanced industrial society than it was in the earlier stage of rapid industrialization. Hence the present more radical policies of reform and restructuring.

Before examining the content and implications of these reforms it is necessary to emphasize again that they are occurring in societies which are socialist in their structure and aims and are likely to remain so for the foreseeable future. By socialist I mean, in the first place, the kind of society defined by Dickinson (1939), pp. 10–11) as

> . . . an economic organization of society in which the material
> means of production are owned by the whole community and
> operated by organs representative of and responsible to the
> community according to a general economic plan, all members of
> the community being entitled to benefit from the results of such
> socialized planned production on the basis of equal rights.

The definition is incomplete in certain respects, since it does not refer to the cultural aims of socialism which Gramsci called the creation of a 'new civilization'; and, as Dickinson himself noted, it also leaves vague two important points: namely, how (in what institutional forms) society is to work the productive equipment that it owns, and exactly how (according to what criteria of service or need, individual or collective consumption) the social product is to be distributed. But it will suffice as a starting point for the present analysis which concentrates upon the economic aspects of socialism and the organization of production. Only in one respect would I make an initial modification by saying that it is the *major* means of production (land and natural resources, large-scale trade and industry, transport and communication) which need to be socially owned, leaving room for private individual or family production in many spheres.

We can now turn to the reforms that are taking place at present in the socialist countries and to an examination of the various projects for combining central planning with markets in economies where most of the material productive forces are, and will continue to be if these societies remain socialist, socially owned. A preliminary observation should be made here: namely, that the economic reforms are necessarily bound up with political reforms, in the sense that, as in other societies, economic renewal can only be successfully accomplished if there is freedom to criticize policies and the actions of public officials, and if political leaders at all levels of the society enjoy the freely expressed confidence of a majority, or at the worst a large part, of the population. The significance of these political conditions will be examined in the next chapter, but their importance should be kept in mind throughout the following discussion.

The current reforms are, in a broad sense, an extension of those which were implemented in Yugoslavia in the 1950s, but in the interim there have been many changes in the world economy, the Yugoslav system itself has encountered serious difficulties, and the present reforms in the socialist world are being undertaken in societies which differ profoundly among themselves in size, resources, history and culture. The fundamental re-examination of the nature of a socialist economy and socialist planning is proceeding, therefore, in the midst of widespread controversy. In what follows I shall not attempt to describe in detail the circumstances and policies of each particular socialist country, but shall concentrate on the principal ideas of the reformers and the theoretical models proposed for a restructured socialist economy, illustrating these ideas and models from the experiences of different countries.[3]

An appropriate starting point is the experience of Yugoslavia, which was the first socialist country to introduce major innovations, through an alternative conception of social ownership, a decentralization of the economy and especially of management, and the development of market relations. The first phase of this new system, up to the early 1960s, was one of considerable achievement in economic growth and rapid industrialization, and in the liberalization of social and cultural life; but in the view of its critics (see especially Golubović, 1986) its further development was compromised by unresolved contradictions in its ideological heritage between the idea of self-management, which became increasingly confined to the economic sphere, and the Leninist view of the 'leading role' of the Communist party in a one-party state. In spite of the reforms of 1965, which established a legal framework for an extended market system (Singleton 1988, pp. 241–4), the economic situation deteriorated rapidly from the mid-1970s, profoundly affected by the rise in oil prices and the economic recession in the West, and has reached crisis proportions in the last few years, with low or zero growth, rapidly increasing unemployment, high inflation, and a massive external debt which now dominates economic policy. The process of liberalization was also halted in an effort to re-establish the authority of the Communist party in the face of radical students' and workers' movements, and the emergence of nationalist movements, although at the same time the ruling party itself became more fragmented as the power of the national states within the Yugoslav federation increased.

The economic problems of Yugoslavia have given rise to a vigorous debate about future policies in which very divergent views have appeared. The essential questions concern the regime of property ownership, the benefits and disadvantages of socialism with markets,[4] and the appropriate planning mechanisms in a restructured socialist economy, but at the same time they are closely related to political issues and have provoked widespread discussion of 'political pluralism' as a means by which citizens can exercise greater influence and control in the formulation and implementation of economic and social policy. These questions have now been clearly posed, in a broadly similar way, in all the European socialist societies, as well as in China, and a variety of solutions have been proposed and partially implemented. First, let us consider property ownership. In all the socialist countries some degree of private ownership of productive resources has always existed, in agriculture and in small-scale manufacturing, trade and services, though it varied considerably in extent from one country to another. The major productive resources, however, are publicly owned in several different forms, as state industries, collective farms, cooperatives, or self-managed enterprises. The latter, as we have seen, were intended to replace state ownership, which concentrates economic power and effective possession of resources in the hands of the leaders and officials of the ruling Communist party, and in the view of many critics creates a new dominant class

(Konrád and Szelény 1979), by a system of social ownership in which workers and employees would effectively participate. However, Golubović (1986, pp. 23–4) argues that, in Yugoslavia, the state has retained its prerogatives to dispose of the means of production and social product, so that ' "social property" oscillates between state usage, which has no legal justification, and "group property" at the level of the enterprise as a visible form of the fragmentation of social property'. As a consequence of this and other factors workers feel that they have less and less say in their enterprise's policy making (p. 20).

The recent reforms in socialist countries have not generally moved towards self-management of the Yugoslav type, but have concentrated upon two issues: a possible extension of private ownership, and greater independence in the management of enterprises by relaxing central planning controls and permitting the development of market relations. As to the first of these issues, it should be noted that in the Soviet Union proposals are being considered for an expansion of private agriculture through the long-term leasing of land from collective farms – whose importance would thereby be diminished – to individuals and families; in Poland, the Solidarity Citizens Committee included in its programme for the parliamentary elections, held in June 1989, a commitment to establish a legal basis for the privatization of state property; and in Hungary, since the introduction of the New Economic Mechanism in 1968, there has been a considerable extension of private economic activity, and this 'second economy' is not only accepted but in some sectors encouraged by the state (Richet 1981, pp. 34–5). The most recent reforms in Hungary which allow the formation of new political parties may well give a further impetus to the second economy.[5]

The expansion of private production, trade and services, has various consequences and implications which I shall examine at a later stage. In the present context its main significance is that it represents one form in which a greater autonomy of enterprises and individual economic agents can be achieved. In short, it is a way of decentralizing economic decision-making, for producers and consumers. Clearly, however, decentralization can also be brought about in other ways, by giving greater independence to publicly owned enterprises and extending the sphere in which market prices determine the levels and types of production and consumption;

from a socialist standpoint it is these alternative routes which are more interesting and important, all the more so because private production and market mechanisms, when they are predominant, themselves create massive economic and social problems.

What we have to examine, therefore, are the models of a decentralized socialist economy which have been worked out, and to some extent, in Hungary and Yugoslavia particularly, implemented in economic reforms. The starting point for the reforms in Eastern Europe has been described by Richet (1981, pp. 24–5) in the following terms:

> According to the centralised conception of economic management, the dynamic behaviour of the economy is governed by the accumulation process, and this in turn is directed by the central authorities (the government and the central planners) acting through a vertically structured organisational system (branch ministries, directorates or associations, and enterprises). In this system the 'central will' largely displaces horizontal regulation through the market mechanism. The resulting process of development relies on extensive growth of the economy and requires for its operation only fairly rough and ready economic measures and indicators. . . .

Richet goes on to say that this hierarchically organized structure 'may well be the most appropriate one when the main tasks of economic policy are concerned with the early stages of accumulation', but it seems less suitable when the economy is more advanced, development becomes more intensive, and 'a more efficient system of information and control is needed'.

Two socialist countries have so far undertaken a fundamental and comprehensive restructuring of the economy – Yugoslavia (where the phase of centralized management was very brief) and Hungary (since the changes initiated in 1968) – and their new economic systems have been influential models for many of the more recent reforms. I have already given some account of the Yugoslav self-management system, and critical evaluations of it, and now turn to examine more specifically the relation between planning and markets which it embodies or is supposed to embody. The theoretical relationship has been clearly formulated by Horvat (1982, ch. 12) who, after rejecting the eclecticism of a 'mixed economy', continues:

> We wish to preserve essential consumer sovereignty because socialism is based on the preferences of the individuals who constitute the society. We also wish to preserve the autonomy of producers, since this is the precondition for self-management. When these are taken together we need a market. But not a laissez-faire market. We need a market that will perform the two functions just stated, neither less nor more. In other words, we need *the market as a planning device* in a strictly defined sphere of priorities . . . [and] *planning as a precondition for an efficient market* . . . in order to increase the economic welfare of the community. (p. 332)

According to this model, planning and markets are complementary, not contradictory, and Horvat goes on to consider the basic functions of a social plan, beyond the formulation of actual plans which have expert and social (normative) components: as a forecasting instrument, as an instrument for coordinating economic decisions and for guiding economic development, and as an obligation for the body that has adopted it and a directive for its organs (pp. 333–4). Having outlined the functions of planning in this way, Horvat then considers the regulatory mechanisms that will be needed, the behaviour of worker-managed firms, the optimum rate of investment, and the basic institutions required for macro-economic organization, comprising a planning bureau, a national bank, a development fund and an arbitration board for incomes and prices.

But the institutions and mechanisms to create an effective connection between planning and markets, as envisaged by Horvat, have not been established in Yugoslavia, and, in the view of Golubović (1986, p. 25), 'Yugoslav society is constantly caught in a dilemma between the *plan* and the *market*, which not only reflects the unclearly defined principles and aims of economic policy, but also is a manifestation of the actual balance of forces in society'; that is to say, of the clash between advocates of centralized bureaucratic planning and those who uphold the absolute validity of market laws. In the present economic crisis, with soaring inflation, very low growth rates, falling real incomes and an increasing polarization into rich and poor, the clash between rival doctrines and policies has become more intense, and it is compounded by national rivalries within the Yugoslav federation.

The question to be explored, which is the subject of very diverse interpretations, is whether the Yugoslav experience demonstrates that there are formidable, even insuperable, difficulties in achieving the integration of planning and markets in any regime of public ownership, or more broadly, in a socialist society. In considering this question, we should remember first that for two decades the Yugoslav system functioned quite effectively, producing high rates of economic growth and an impressive development of social and cultural life. The turning point came with the oil price rises and the Western recession of the early 1970s, which also affected other East European countries. It may be argued that the subsequent economic decline is due in large measure to the failure of planning to deal effectively with the consequences of these events, and in particular with the massive growth of external indebtedness, which has also notably affected the Polish and Hungarian economies. It is certain that the economic development of Yugoslavia and other socialist societies has been adversely affected in some respects – whatever the initial advantages may have been, or seemed to be – by their close links, in foreign trade and investment, with the capitalist world, and by the failure of policy-makers to take due account of the cycle of growth and recession in capitalist economies which is, after all, at the heart of Marxist economic analysis.

This failure may itself be attributed in part to the weakness of political leadership, in conditions where, according to Golubović, self-management has been largely subordinated to bureaucratic control and is more an ideology than a reality, and there is a consequent loss of enthusiasm, a general stagnation in which no clear conception of long-term development has been formulated. What is evident so far is that the economic situation has deteriorated more rapidly since the extension of market relations, although, as I have said, there were also powerful external forces at work. Some critics of the present system, at the opposite pole from reformers such as Golubović, nevertheless consider that a solution of the difficulties lies in a further extension of markets; but although this might perhaps stimulate some kinds of economic growth, it would also almost certainly increase the disparity between rich and poor and perpetuate high levels of unemployment, as has happened in many capitalist countries of Western Europe. The alternative, as Horvat proposes, is to create more sophisticated, clearly defined, and efficient planning institutions,

and at the same time to give some new stimulus to self-management, or more generally to self-government and democratization in
all spheres, which seems unmistakably to involve the development
of a pluralistic political system.

The experience of Hungary over the past two decades has been
similar in some respects to that of Yugoslavia. The New Economic
Mechanism which came into force in January 1968, after three
years of careful preliminary research, was intended to decentralize
economic decision-making and to introduce elements of market
competition. The main feature of the reform was

. . . its abolition of the standard Soviet-type procedures of oper-
ative annual planning. Enterprises were no longer to receive *any*
compulsory indicators from higher levels of the planning hier-
archy. Five-year and annual plans were still to be formulated
within the central agencies . . . but annual plans would no longer
be implemented by means of direct instructions to enterprises.
Instead, plans were implemented indirectly by means of the so-
called economic regulators, which influenced the financial environment within which enterprises operated. Enterprises themselves
were supposed to respond to market signals, essentially the price
system, in order to maximise their profits. (Hare, Radice and
Swain, p. 14)

But, in 1971, an element of labour direction was introduced, and in
1974 central control over investment plans was strengthened,
because the release of market forces led to problems in the markets
for labour and investment; and in later years there were further
measures of re-centralization, mainly, as Hare *et al.* (p. 15) note, 'in
response to the economic effects of the dramatic rise in the price of
oil and other raw materials in 1974–5, coupled with the Western
recession [which] led to a serious deterioration in the terms of trade
and the balance of payments'.

The reform policy, however, was only temporarily interrupted; in
January 1980 much of the original mechanism was reinstated, and
since then further radical changes have been undertaken, including
monetary and fiscal reforms which introduced personal income tax
and value added tax, and most recently the first steps in the
development of a multi-party political system. The Hungarian
reforms, however, have not followed the Yugoslav model of
workers' self-management; on the contrary, they are much more

individualistic and market-orientated in their approach. As I noted earlier, the 'second economy' is already a major element in economic life, and the economic reform plan adopted in 1988 envisages the development of a 'genuine market economy' in which the share of the private sector might rise to some 30 per cent; there would be more extensive shareholding (in state enterprises too, though in a collective form) and a more widely functioning stock exchange, closer to the Western capitalist model, would develop. The introduction of personal income tax was itself an 'individualizing' measure, partly in response to the growth of income inequality resulting from private enterprise in the second economy, and it was strongly opposed by critics (not necessarily advocates of more centralized planning) who saw it as a substantial departure from the values of a socialist society.

It is too early yet to judge the economic results of the Hungarian reforms. Hare, Radice and Swain (1981, p. 20) refer to their 'apparently limited impact' on economic performance, but go on to say that 'without the reforms performance might have deteriorated substantially'. But it is evident, in any case, that so far Hungary has not done notably better than some other socialist countries (and especially the German Democratic Republic)[6] which rely to a much greater extent upon central planning, and the modest improvement in the socialist economies in 1988 was not more marked in Hungary than elsewhere.

In China, the economic changes since 1976 have been much more sweeping than in the East European countries, and, in the view of some commentators and socialist critics, can be regarded as the first stages in a process of 'restoring capitalism'.[7] The main elements in this process have been the rapid development of market mechanisms which profoundly modify the social objectives of the planning system and result in growing inequality, a 'decollectivization' of agriculture which increasingly favours rich private farmers, and the 'open door' policy with regard to foreign capital, in the form of joint ventures and extra-territorial 'special economic zones', which promotes development above all in the foreign trade sectors of the economy. The outcome so far of these economic changes is unclear. China is still going through a period of economic turmoil, in which economic growth declined sharply from 1979 to 1981, but has recovered since then, though it is still not as high as in the period 1965–78.[8] Clearly, the economic situation of China (and of other

Third World socialist countries) differs greatly from that in the countries of Eastern Europe which are, in varying degrees, industrially developed societies; and the present Chinese reforms can be viewed to some extent as a temporary expedient similar to the NEP in the Soviet Union in the period 1921-7.

At the same time there are some general similarities in the economic reforms now being implemented in most of the socialist countries; and it seems unlikely, for example, that the Chinese version of NEP will be followed by a period of Stalinist-type planning. To put the matter in another way, 'socialism with markets' seems to be here to stay, and it is welcomed by most socialist thinkers as well as by the overwhelming majority of the population in socialist countries. But it is not without its own problems and dubious aspects, as the preceding discussion has indicated, and it will be useful now to attempt a provisional summary of the main issues.

First, the question of markets has to be distinguished clearly from that of the ownership of means of production. The markets we are talking about, in a socialist society, are markets in which socially owned enterprises are major participants. Without social ownership on an extensive scale there can be, in my view, no socialism. But this still leaves a large sphere in which small-scale private production can flourish - in the arts and cultural activities generally (including book publishing), in services of all kinds to consumers, in local trade, and in some areas of agriculture. The case of agriculture is particularly interesting because there seems to be a fairly widespread agreement that the economic reforms should begin with agriculture,[9] and that this involves to a greater or lesser extent a privatization of agricultural production. But this question needs careful examination. In the first place, small-scale private production is not necessarily more efficient; for example, in Poland, where most agricultural production is in private hands, it is not notably efficient and indeed seems to be afflicted by the same confusion and *malaise* as the rest of the Polish economy. Second, while state collective farms may be inefficient in the Soviet Union they are not so in Czechoslovakia, as some internal critics of aspects of the reform process have pointed out; and more generally it should be pointed out that the supply of basic, and not so basic, foodstuffs in advanced societies in fact depends upon large-scale production, as is shown by the development of agri-business in the capitalist world, which in turn depends very much upon the supply of industrial products. The reform of agriculture in socialist countries therefore requires, above all, more efficient management of collective farms, the decentralization of decision-making and the introduction of elements of self-management, together with a better supply of modern machinery (which of course depends upon the success of the reforms in industrial production); but this still leaves an important area in which production by individuals, families and small- or medium-size cooperatives is appropriate and desirable.

A second major point is that markets in a socialist society should be conceived, in Horvat's sense, as a 'planning device' within a general economic plan, and hence regulated in accordance with social objectives. The problem is how to accomplish this regulation effectively. There is, according to Ellman (1989, p. 81), who cites studies relating to the Hungarian reforms, a 'regulation illusion' which consists in 'the idea that enterprise behaviour can easily be controlled by the planners by manipulation of certain regulators (e.g. prices, taxes, laws, etc.)', which turns out to be more difficult than was imagined, for several reasons: 'enterprises react to a whole complex of economic, social and political factors', 'it is impossible to develop a completely watertight system of rules and regulations', and 'the goals of the enterprises [may be] other than those hoped for by the planners', leading to unexpected reactions. Ellman *(ibid.)* then suggests that the critique of the regulation illusion is 'analogous to the rational expectations critique of the Keynesian belief in the easy controllability of the economy'. What can be concluded from this is that regulation in modern, complex, rapidly changing economies, either capitalist or socialist, is difficult and imperfect; and it remains to be seen whether the current reforms in the socialist countries will achieve some less imperfect regulatory system. In principle, this should be possible given the existence of a more comprehensive planning system, and it is certainly desirable in order to attain the overall social objectives and to counter the well-known adverse consequences of a market economy.

Two particular issues are closely connected with the development of greater enterprise autonomy, market competition and a more indirect system of planning and regulation. One is that of improving management efficiency, and more widely of encouraging a kind of socialist entrepreneurship which would bring about more rapid technological innovation.[10] In this respect, as with other features of the economy, there are considerable differences between socialist countries, and in the GDR the quality of industrial management is already high by international standards.[11] No doubt, cultural and historical factors play an important part in these differences, but in general the quality of management depends on incentives (not only of a pecuniary kind) and on careful planning (of training, career structures, etc.). However, management efficiency is not the only factor in raising productivity, increasing the rate of innovation and promoting more rapid economic growth, and a second issue concerns the response, and the attitudes, of workers. Here, too, incentives of various kinds are required, among them opportunities for greater participation in decision-making through reforms which may tend towards an effective system of self-managed enterprises.

Not all the socialist societies are moving towards a self-management system (which has, as we have seen, its own problems), but there is an unmistakable desire for, and growth of, participation at all levels of society. Thus, there is a third issue involved in the present reforms: namely, the development of a greater 'openness' in society accompanying the restructuring of the economy and now widely regarded as being crucially important for the success of the whole reforming process. The economic changes, it is recognized, require a new political climate in which the population can have greater confidence in their leaders, express their wishes and criticisms more freely and effectively, and take a larger part in the determination of social policy; for it is only in such a climate that a new enthusiasm, animation and readiness to innovate can flourish.

The speed of political change varies from one country to another, but in most of them there is now greater freedom of expression, and in some, freer elections have been held or are to be held. The emergence of various social movements and political groupings has been tolerated or fully recognized in several countries, and there is widespread discussion of the creation of a multi-party system, which is already far advanced in Hungary. All these changes diminish the absolute power of the Communist party, which has existed in the Soviet Union since 1917 and in most other socialist countries since the end of the Second World War; and they point perhaps towards an eventual socialist political system in which coalitions of various independent parties are a normal feature of government, while other parties function effectively as a critical opposition. Some characteristics of such a system are indeed already appearing. But the greater 'openness' of the socialist societies involves much more than just the formation of new political parties. It represents, as some observers have noted, a recreation of 'civil society'; that is to say, a revival of the network of autonomous associations of all kinds in which citizens can pursue their interests, express their ideas and construct a style of life, free from government intervention and regulation (within the limits set by law). And this development of civil society is also of vital importance for renewing the active involvement of citizens in the whole process of reform.

Needless to say, the present radical changes in the economy and society are not proceeding entirely smoothly, or without producing some unwelcome side-effects. The greater freedom for new political movements, which has been welcomed as a means of increasing public participation in and democratic control over policy-making, has stimulated the growth of nationalist movements in some federal states (notably in Yugoslavia and, to a lesser extent, in the Soviet Union), and these may become extremely disruptive, without making any significant contribution to economic renewal. The rise of nationalism is no doubt connected with economic dissatisfactions (as has been the case in Western capitalist countries; for example, the Quebec independence movement in Canada in the 1960s), but it also has a very strong cultural component which is only distantly related to the main intentions of the current reforms and is often backward-looking. From another aspect, however, the nationalist movements illustrate a more general phenomenon, which is the unavoidable proliferation of special interest groups in a more open society. These interests, depending on the context, may be provincial, national, regional, occupational or cultural, or some combination of them; and it is already evident that among the interests at work are those of the old-style bureaucracy. Overall, therefore, the process of change in the socialist countries is likely to be a turbulent one, and those who are committed to reform – to the creation of prosperous, democratic socialist societies – can only hope (with a certain degree of confidence indeed) that what is now taking place will turn out to be, in Schumpeter's phrase, 'a gale of creative destruction'.

It is too early as yet to pronounce any kind of definitive verdict on the merits of a more market-orientated socialist economy. The preceding discussion shows that there are still many difficulties to be resolved, and there are also sharply contrasting experiences with regard to the scope of central planning and markets respectively; for example, between the GDR and Hungary. Certainly we are still very far from possessing a convincing theoretical model, let alone any functioning practical example, of an 'ideal', or even greatly improved socialist economy. Nevertheless, I think some tentative conclusions can be reached at this stage – drawing on the discussion in this and earlier chapters – about the results of central planning[12] and its lessons for the future development of socialist economies with markets, before proceeding in the next chapter to study more closely the major problems of socialism at present.

First, it should be clearly stated that centrally planned socialist economies have undoubtedly been successful in several important respects: in mobilizing resources for development, especially rapid industrialization, and in some periods attaining very high rates of growth, as well as achieving greater economic stability than is the case in capitalist countries. But they have not caught up with, let alone surpassed, the major capitalist countries which, in contrast with the inter-war period, have been remarkably successful since the Second World War – inexplicably perhaps, unless one takes into account the more extensive economic planning and regulation, and greatly increased public expenditure, which they also have introduced. And since the mid-1970s the socialist countries have gone through a period of stagnation, or even decline, which is the proximate source of the reform movement.

The main objective of all the reforms is to decentralize economic decision-making by giving more freedom and responsibility to managers and workers, in order to increase efficient use of resources, stimulate technological innovation, raise productivity and especially improve the supply of consumer goods and services. This necessarily involves the growth of market relations, in which enterprises and other agencies negotiate their own contracts with other bodies. It does not, however, necessitate any considerable expansion of private production, since socially owned enterprises can operate perfectly well in a market situation; and the scale of private production is a matter to be determined on other criteria, as I argued earlier, and as many socialists have long recognized.

On the other hand, the extension of market relations needs also to be regulated within the framework of a general planning process, in order to preserve the benefits of economic stability and long-term projects for investment and growth, and also to counter such ill effects of market forces as growing inequality or the spread of an unbridled acquisitiveness. The major problem, then, is to devise a new and more sophisticated planning machinery, a task which should be much easier in the intellectual climate of debate and criticism which is now emerging. The fundamental issues that need to be considered form the subject of the next two chapters.

Notes

1. See the discussion in Chapter 2 above, and also Széll (1988, section 2).
2. I have discussed the theory of 'organized capitalism' and the related theory of 'state monopoly capitalism' in Bottomore (1985, ch. 5).
3. A general economic history of Eastern Europe is in course of publication by the Clarendon Press, and vol. III, edited by M. C. Kaser (1986), provides a good account of institutional changes in these planned economies up to 1975. There is also much valuable information in the monographs published by the Research Project 'Crises in Soviet-type systems', and I shall refer to individual monographs at relevant points. In addition, there is, of course, a large and growing literature on individual countries upon which I shall draw in the appropriate contexts.
4. In the following discussion I shall use the term 'socialism with markets' suggested by Tomlinson (see above, p.78) which seems to me a more accurate description of a socialist view of the role of markets than the more commonly used 'market socialism'.
5. According to the 'approximate and incomplete data' assembled by Gábor and Galasi (1981, pp. 48–9), this second economy was already very large by the end of the 1970s, absorbing the labour of about one million people out of an economically active population of 5.2 million.
6. According to Ellman (1989, p. 67): 'In the mid 1980s the GDR was a stable welfare state with the highest living standards in the CMEA. Its macro-economic performance was marked by steady growth and stable prices, at any rate as measured by official statistics. These statistics overstated its actual performance. Nevertheless, compared to the other CMEA countries, its achievements were real and impressive.' Specific historical and cultural factors have affected the development of the GDR, but the experience still shows that rational central planning can be very effective in an advanced industrial society.
7. See especially Chossudovsky (1986).

8. Chossudovsky (1986, pp. 127-8).
9. See Ellman (1989, pp. 76-7).
10. The relatively low rate of technological innovation in the Soviet economy has been an important factor in the economic stagnation of the past decade. See the discussion in Chapter 5, and the studies by Berliner (1988) cited there.
11. See Granick (1975, p. 215) and the discussion by Ellman (1989, p. 67).
12. See also the discussion in Ellman (1989, ch. 10).

7

Problems of socialism today

The idea of 'burying socialism' is a fantasy of some conservative politicians, mainly in Britain and the United States. In the wider world there are many socialist or socialistic[1] societies, of diverse kinds, which for the most part function adequately and in some cases very well.[2] Like all forms of society, however, they have evolved historically and continue to evolve, encountering fresh problems at every stage. In the preceding chapters I have discussed the socialist project from its formulation in the ideas particularly of the Utopian thinkers and the Marxist socialists, through the debates about central planning in the 1930s and the experience of planning in the Soviet Union, to the renewed discussions and experiments of the post-war period, involving above all the restructuring of socialist economies to encompass both planning and markets. Against this background I propose now to consider some of the fundamental problems which need to be resolved, if the socialist renaissance of the past decade is actually to lead towards the creation of a new civilization.

Some preliminary comments are in order. First, it is necessary to distinguish between the kinds of society which I have called 'socialist' and 'socialistic', the former group comprising the Soviet Union and the countries of Eastern Europe, China and some Third World countries, the latter including those countries, mainly in Western Europe but also in the Third World, which have had for longer or shorter periods socialist or social democratic governments committed to an extension of public ownership, a high level of public expenditure, and some degree of central planning. The problems confronting these two groups of countries are different in nature and will be treated separately. It will also be necessary, as we proceed, to define more closely the basic characteristics of the two groups, as well as any major variations within them.

The socialist countries

They are socialist, first, in the fundamental sense which has been the distinctive feature of the whole socialist movement since its beginnings: namely, that the major means of production (other than human labour) are socially owned. But they are also socialist, in a second and later sense, in being 'planned' societies.[3] Third, they began with the aspiration to create a broad economic and social equality among their citizens and to liberate the individual human being, or as Marx and some later Marxists expressed it, to 'end alienation'; but in these respects they failed signally (though Yugoslavia was an exception) during the Stalinist period and less blatantly in the following decades until the recent reforms were initiated.

The importance of social ownership is that it embodies one of the central values of socialism; the attainment of a practical form of collective self-determination in which a community of free and equal citizens decides consciously and deliberately upon the general framework of its economic and social life, and is no longer dominated by a particular class – the owners of capital. But the actual realization of this value – which has been expressed in diverse forms, from Marx's 'associated producers' to 'self-management' and 'participatory democracy' – encounters, as the historical experience of socialism in the twentieth century should teach us, immense and fundamental difficulties. In the first place, individual citizens or groups of citizens may want very different things which are, to say the least, difficult to reconcile. Second, it is impossible that a community of several million people, such as even the smaller modern nations are, should decide and act collectively in a direct and immediate way; hence some kind of representative system must necessarily be created (though it may take many forms, with varying degrees of participation). A representative system not only gives expression to existing particular interests, but also produces new interests and divisions out of which there may emerge either a compromise negotiated between different groups or an authoritarian solution imposed by a particular group.

These are the problems, long familiar in political philosophy, of the 'general will', on which Hobhouse (1918, p. 126), with a clear awareness of sociological realities, commented that 'the real objection to the term is that in so far as it is will it is not general, and in so far as it is general it is not will'.[4] The same problems have been restated in a different way by Hayek in the course of his long-sustained critique of socialism, and most fully in his recent work (Hayek 1982), where he expounds his ideal of a 'spontaneous order' as the only form of society that can provide the condition of freedom, 'in which each can use his knowledge for his purposes' (vol. II, p. 56), in opposition to the vision of a rationally planned society which has as its goal the achievement of social justice. The latter, he argues, is doomed to failure since 'society, in the strict sense in which it must be distinguished from the apparatus of government, is incapable of acting for a specific purpose' (vol. II, p. 64), precisely because it does not have a 'general will' or a general consciousness in which the dispersed knowledge and purposes of individuals can be brought together. It is on these grounds that Hayek, in his more strictly economic writings, always refers to the decisions of central planning agencies as 'arbitrary'.[5]

I shall argue later that a socialist society in which there is social ownership of the major means of production does not need to rest upon the notion of a general will or some kind of universal consensus; but before embarking on that subject it is necessary to consider the role of central planning, which has become the second principal feature of socialist economies, and equally a principal target of anti-socialist criticism. The idea of planning was implicit in almost all socialist thought from the end of the nineteenth century,[6] and necessarily so, because it was (or appeared to be) the only alternative to capitalist markets as a mechanism for coordinating the economic system as a whole. But it was only after the creation in 1917 of the first socialist society that central planning came to occupy a major place in the definition of socialism and that the idea of a 'planned society' began to be widely diffused, as Durbin (1949) and many others recognized. From the 1930s onwards socialism became virtually identified with central planning, and planning itself acquired a new significance as the main element in the project of creating a 'rational society' in which the instability, waste, frustration and inequality of a capitalist economy would be overcome. Hayek (1982) is right, therefore, in tracing one important strand in twentieth-century socialist thought to the spread of a rationalist view of the world, aided by the rapid growth of the natural sciences; to which he opposes his own conception of the evolution of human society as a largely unconscious process.[7]

We are not concerned here with the wider questions of social theory raised by Hayek's critique of a rational and planned society, but only with what we can learn from this and similar critiques, as well as from historical experience and the more recent socialist debates, about the problems and limitations of planning.[8] Some of these issues have been examined in the previous chapter, among them the growth of bureaucracy, which may result, on one side, in the diffusion of a cautious and conservative outlook and the stifling of enterprise and innovation, and on the other, in the emergence of a new privileged stratum which dominates society; and also the difficulties experienced by the kind of central planning which attempts to control directly, and in detail, the activities of individual enterprises in an advanced, complex and rapidly changing economy.

But there is still a more general question to be examined which concerns both social ownership and planning, and takes us back to the ideas of the nineteenth-century socialists, in a period when the actual institutions and mechanisms that would need to be created in a socialist economy had scarcely begun to be considered. In discussing Utopian thought in the novels of Bellamy and Morris (see Chapter 1 above), I observed that their vision of the functioning of a new society presupposed a radical transformation of human nature, as a result of which the sentiments favourable to peaceful cooperation, social responsibility and non-acquisitiveness would come to predominate in shaping human behaviour; and for all the disclaimers that were made, Utopian ideas also profoundly affected the views of Marx and later Marxists, as well as other socialists. Not the least of the consequences was that the establishment of a socialist economy was regarded, at least tacitly, as a relatively simple and uncomplicated process, and with rare exceptions was not seriously discussed until the 1920s.

The idea of a transformed human nature still plays an important part in socialist thought today, although it is very rarely subjected to any profound analysis.[9] From one aspect it may be conceived as the statement of 'an ideal end which gives a sense of direction to human self-creation in history' (Marković 1983, p. 217), and in this form it remains an essential and inexpugnable element in the movement towards socialism.[10] But it is sheer folly for socialists to embark upon the construction of a socialist economy and society as if that ideal end had already been attained. Human nature as it actually exists is complex, its bounds and possibilities still obscure and very diversely interpreted, and at the same time – so obviously and yet so frequently disregarded – extremely variable between individuals, although it is also historically mutable and there is no absurdity in supposing that in a socialist society what may be called 'average' human nature would eventually manifest itself in more cooperative, less aggressive forms of behaviour. A realistic form of socialism, or what Nove (1983) has termed 'feasible socialism', cannot begin, however, from the unreal presumption that in a socialist society – as it might exist in any foreseeable future – all individuals, or even a substantial majority of them, will be devoted to the public good, that there will be no individuals who single-mindedly and ruthlessly seek power, wealth and privilege, or that no clashes of individual or group interest will occur and require mediation.

These rather general and abstract considerations have a very direct and practical bearing on the problems of the existing socialist societies, for it has been a constant theme in the criticisms (both internal and external) of their economies in the past few decades that they are relatively inefficient in their use of resources, insufficiently enterprising and innovative, and have not moved rapidly enough from 'extensive' to 'intensive' development. The current reforms are intended to overcome these deficiencies, above all by a decentralization of economic decision-making, so that managers and workers in individual enterprises have greater independence and responsibility, and also more incentives (which need not be exclusively monetary) to produce efficiently. Such a decentralized economy implies the existence of a market, and an element of competition among producers, which itself would be a stimulus to greater efficiency.

Such wide-ranging and fundamental changes are bound to

produce difficulties of their own: uncertainty, a degree of confusion, and resistance from some individuals and groups whose particular interests are threatened, as well as specific problems of unemployment and the development of new kinds of inequality. The difficulties can only be countered by the retention of an effective planning system, which will, however, assume a different character, so that 'greater use is to be made of indirect financial "levers" such as prices, taxes, and credit, in place of detailed output assignments and input authorizations enforced by central allocation of supplies' (Bornstein 1973, p. 8).[11] There is a particular need for central planning in respect of investment, and as Marschak (1973, p. 58) comments, 'whatever the defects of a centralized scheme for determining the volume and composition of the economy's investment, at least only one agency has control over the scheme and can modify it if it appears to perform badly'. The optimum mix of planning and markets is not something that can be determined by reference to a developed theoretical model or blueprint, because that does not exist and is perhaps unattainable in conditions of imperfect knowledge of all the relevant data, and it can therefore only be approached through a pragmatic strategy and continuous learning process. This is the course that seems to have been generally adopted in the socialist countries, producing diverse types of reform measures; and some time must elapse before its results can be properly assessed. There is no reason to suppose, however, that the problems encountered by the new-style socialist economies will be any greater than those (which are well known) of capitalist economies. In my estimation they are likely to be less serious and more easily resolved, though there will be considerable differences between countries in their degree of success, just as there are among capitalist countries.

The issue of decentralization, expanded market relations and a new type of planning (which will also, of course, embrace local and regional planning) is quite separate from that of public or private ownership of economic resources, although the two things have frequently been associated, or strictly connected, in the arguments of anti-socialist critics (for example, Mises). Publicly or socially owned enterprises[12] can operate perfectly well in a system of market relations with central planning, and the questions which may be raised about them are basically of two kinds. First, what can or should be the extent of private production of goods and services in

a socialist economy? I have already made clear my view, which is
that of many socialists, including Marxists such as Kautsky, that
private production will have an important place in any realistically
conceivable socialist economy (as it has done in practice in the
existing socialist societies). Its advantages seem evident as an
adjunct to large-scale industrial and agricultural production, the
administration of public utilities, and the provision of infrastructural services such as health and education. In many spheres
(small-scale trade, restaurants, market gardening, bookshops, some
publishing, small-scale building and repair work, and so on) private
producers can probably respond more quickly to consumer needs
and provide more convenient services, and they may also have an
important role as innovators. There is not, I think, any way of
deciding in advance for any lengthy period of time exactly what the
extent of private production should be, and in this case, too, a
pragmatic approach seems advisable, though there should be
restrictions (as there have been in the socialist countries) on the
number of employees that a private producer can have. Furthermore, it should not be overlooked that much small-scale production and provision of services can be undertaken by cooperatives
(as it has been) with the same advantage.

The second major question that has frequently been raised with
reference to publicly owned enterprises concerns their efficiency
and ability to innovate, which is related in most of the discussions
to the question of incentives for both management and workers.
This is a matter which is still difficult to decide in an exact or
convincing way, and I shall confine myself to some general
considerations and a very tentative judgement. First, it should be
clear that we are dealing, in the case of the socialist countries, only
with a *relative* inefficiency, and even then not in all cases: the GDR,
for example, has a relatively efficient socialized agriculture
(whatever may be the case in the Soviet Union) and industry, and
its GNP per capita is probably higher than that of Britain, which is
admittedly one of the least successful capitalist countries. More
generally, it is widely recognized that the socialist countries as a
whole (with few exceptions) were very successful in earlier periods
in achieving rapid industrialization, and major technological innovation in some spheres. Only in the past two decades have their
economies (or most of them) experienced a relative stagnation, at a
time when most of the capitalist economies were maintaining, until

recently, their previous rates of growth.

In principle, there seems to be no reason that publicly owned enterprises and public services should not be as efficient as those which are privately owned and managed, particularly in the new economic conditions where enterprises have more autonomy and there is a degree of competition between them. The experience of many West European countries shows that, in practice, publicly owned or cooperative enterprises in a capitalist economy (in manufacturing, transport, and public utilities) can operate at a high level of efficiency; and there are also examples, as I have noted at various points, of socialist economies, or particular sectors within them, which are efficiently and successfully managed. Nevertheless, there are two considerations which suggest that central planners and political leaders in a socialist society may be led to opt for a somewhat lower level of efficiency, in order to attain other social goals.

First, the drive for greater efficiency, and especially the growth of productivity through technological innovation in a more competitive economic climate, may come into conflict with the basic socialist policy of full employment. In Yugoslavia, unemployment has long been a problem, and similar problems are now appearing in some other socialist countries. It is very unlikely that these societies will accept a growth of unemployment to the levels that exist in many capitalist countries, and consequently they will not readily permit the closure of less efficient enterprises, unless alternative employment is available. In the longer term, a solution may be found in the expansion of new occupations, particularly in the service sector of the economy, and in a steady reduction of working hours, which should in any case be a major element in socialist policy, accompanying the growth of productivity. But here also there is no blueprint to follow, and no easy or cost-free options. Policy-making will have to proceed largely in piecemeal fashion, dealing with specific problems as they arise, and, as I have suggested, there may well be some deliberate sacrifice of efficiency, at least in the short term, at the enterprise level for the sake of the human and social benefits of full employment. Moreover, even from the economic aspect it may be argued that a system which maintains full employment is in one sense *more* efficient than an economy which wastes a substantial part of its labour force through unemployment.[13]

The second major issue is the role of competition in a socialist society. On one side, increased competition between independently managed enterprises in a market situation is seen as a means of increasing efficiency, encouraging innovation, and ensuring, in particular, a better, more varied supply of consumer goods. On the other side, it is evident that the competitive spirit, certainly in its more extreme forms, is incompatible with the distinctive emphasis that is placed, in all forms of socialist thought, on the value of cooperation and the good of the community. It is not a matter, however, of choosing one option and excluding the other entirely, but of exploring the terms on which they can coexist in a socialist society. In the first place, some degree of rivalry and competition seems inescapable in human societies, arising from a universal desire for personal or group achievement, which may manifest itself in many different spheres. But individual achievement does not exclude cooperation, and is indeed often facilitated by it; and on the other hand, where it does take the form of rivalry, it has always to be circumscribed and regulated in some way, in order to maintain the unity of a larger whole, or more deliberately to attain what is conceived as a 'good society'. In particular, economic competition and the rivalry between nation states need to be restrained, because of the undesirable consequences which may come from their being allowed a free rein, though the possibility of effective restraint depends to a great extent upon the strength of the interests – of class or national ambition – that are involved.

At all events, the celebration of the unalloyed virtues of competition indulged in by latter-day advocates of *laissez-faire* capitalism, which I have criticized elsewhere (Bottomore 1986-7), is totally alien to socialist thought, and the practice of competition in this manner is incompatible with a socialist form of society. There are two issues here which deserve particular attention. One concerns the kind of society which is created when individual achievement comes to be judged primarily in terms of the acquisition of wealth, and money dominates social life. In such a society many other human values are sacrificed to what is seen as the motor of economic progress, and the result for some is deprivation of the basic requirements of a civilized life, for many more the sense of living in a dull, oppressive, tawdry and uncreative world. Among the values most conspicuously sacrificed is that of an agreeable and safe environment, and this constitutes the second of the issues to be faced in socialist societies, and by socialist parties everywhere. Few people now doubt that the natural environment of human societies is seriously endangered, but it cannot be said that the existing socialist countries have so far been notably enlightened in their environmental ideas and practices. Like other industrial societies, and for specific reasons which I discussed in an earlier chapter, they have focused their attention almost exclusively upon overall economic growth, in a climate of opinion where comparisons between countries tend to be made largely in terms of rates of growth and standards of material life. Of course, the latter are important. One of the fundamental aims of socialism has been to provide a decent and comfortable life for all citizens, and steadily to improve the material conditions of life through economic growth (which some socialist countries have, in recent times, conspicuously failed to do). But this is not, and could not be, the only aim; and what can reasonably be expected at a stage when basic material needs – by the standards of the present time – can be adequately met, is that the socialist countries should demonstrate a superior ability, not to increase without limit the flow of material goods, but to create a society which is satisfying in all its aspects: without extremes of wealth and poverty, culturally creative, enjoying extensive leisure, caring for its natural environment, and encouraging in its citizens an active participation in public life and commitment to the public good.

The problems involved in restructuring the socialist economies are multiform and complex, and the process of solving them is likely to be long and difficult. In this process, as I have argued, what is important is not the question of ownership (although in some spheres it may be desirable to expand small-scale private production) or the excessive promotion of competition, but the decentralization of economic decision-making by giving enterprises greater independence in a controlled system of market relations (which of course implies an element of competition) and developing new, indirect methods of planning the economy as a whole. But the economic changes, as I have made clear, are bound up with political reforms; and throughout the socialist world these two aspects are closely associated in the ideas of the reformers. The new economic policies necessarily provoke widespread political debate, and they also have political consequences, for example in diminishing the power of bureaucratic organizations (including sections of the party bureaucracy), or what Konrád and Szelényi (1979) refer to as the new intellectual class of 'rational redistributors'. More generally, the success of the economic reforms depends to a very great extent upon awakening public enthusiasm and commitment, and this can only happen if there is opportunity to express freely and effectively ideas and criticisms.

In an important sense the whole reform movement can properly be described as a process of democratization, coming very late, one may think, in the development of socialist society. In the political sphere this requires free elections, a multi-party system to the extent that major differences of interest or aim become manifest, an electoral system (including some form of proportional representation) which allows all significant interests and aspirations to be represented in government, freedom of political activity for social movements, groups and individuals within the limits set by the rule of law, and all those ancillary, essential freedoms embodied in a free press, a bill of rights, and a pervasive democratic spirit in public life which, among other things, protects the rights of minorities. In such conditions a socialist democracy would show itself superior in many respects to even the most democratic capitalist countries, where the pervasive influence of wealth (not least in the mass media), the tendency towards a trivialization of politics (political meetings as circuses), and in some cases electoral systems which produce very unrepresentative governments, all tend to limit the extent of democratic participation.[14] This is not all, however. From the beginning, socialists conceived democracy as a form of social life which should be developed as widely as possible beyond the narrowly defined political sphere; hence the use of the term 'social democracy' by socialist parties. The economic reforms in the socialist countries have therefore also, in this sense, a directly political significance. Decentralization itself will bring somewhat greater control over their immediate conditions of life to the personnel of individual enterprises, because they will no longer be directly subordinate to regional or central bureaucratic organizations; but the process may nevertheless have very different outcomes depending upon how the internal structure of the enterprises evolves. It is possible, for example, that the system of management will be reconstructed in such a way that a new élite of technocrats and managers will emerge in the economy as a whole and begin to acquire political power (or even that a new class of capitalists will appear). Alternatively, the process of democratization may lead in a more socialist direction towards some kind of self-management which, for all its current difficulties in Yugoslavia, has shown itself, over a fairly long period, to be a viable, and in earlier periods very successful, type of economic organization. The restructuring of the socialist economies is, therefore, not only profoundly affected by political reforms, but is itself a political as well as an economic phenomenon, on which the socialist future of these countries depends.

The 'socialistic' countries

The countries, mainly in Western Europe, which I have called 'socialistic', face problems which are very different from those in the socialist countries, although some issues are of common concern, in particular the forms which public ownership (or control) of productive resources, and economic planning, should take in the future. In these countries the movement towards socialism has been gradual, often checked (or in the case of Britain during the past ten years violently reversed) by the advent of conservative governments, although Sweden and Austria constitute an exception in this respect.[15] These two countries can indeed be regarded as particularly socialistic, in several senses, and I shall begin with a brief account of the main features of their economies and social policies.

In Sweden, the socialist party (SAP) has been in power almost continuously since 1932, and in that time has brought about substantial changes in Swedish society, especially since 1945. The 1950s and 1960s were decades of rapid economic growth, as they were generally in Western Europe, and in Sweden they were also marked by a sustained movement towards socialism, in the sense of greater economic equality, more industrial democracy, and a substantial expansion of the public sector. The 1970s, following the oil crisis, brought harsher economic conditions throughout the Western world, with weaker economic growth and rising unemployment, but Sweden has weathered this critical period better than most countries (and notably better than Britain), while maintaining its socialistic policies. As Rydén and Bergström (1982, p. 1) note, the democratization of working life, increasing the power of the unions and diminishing that of corporate owners, the expansion of the public sector, more public regulation and participation in industry, have all continued; and they conclude that this 'has meant increased importance for everything we refer to when talking of the quality of life – a better environment, more leisure, increased possibilities for making the decisions that affect one's life. But it has also meant continued centralization, bureaucratization, intensified efficiency and a sense of alienation in the individual facing large private and public bureaucracies'. They go on to discuss the major problem of the disproportion between the demands on society and its productive capacity (especially if there were a serious energy crisis), and its relation to the traditional system of wage formation through free negotiation.[16] Nevertheless, while recognizing the seriousness of the economic problems, they also point out that 'the international economic crisis of the 1970s touched the average Swedish consumer relatively mildly [and] open unemployment never rose above 2.5 per cent', and conclude that, overall, 'Swedish society and the Swedish economy – the welfare state – have proved enormously strong against the instability and crises of the 1970s' (*ibid.*, p. 8). It is noteworthy also that, during this period of economic difficulties, the government pressed ahead with a project that would gradually extend the collective ownership of productive resources through the employee investment funds (which will be discussed in the next chapter), and thus maintained, to some extent, the impetus of the movement towards socialism.

In Austria the implementation of socialist policies on a national scale is a post-war phenomenon, although the socialist party (SPÖ) could draw upon the earlier experience of the socialist administration of Vienna in the years 1918–34, and it has occurred in a different context. For historical reasons, there has been a considerable expansion of public ownership of industry and financial institutions, beginning with the nationalization of Austria's largest bank, the Credit-Anstalt, following its collapse in 1931, and continuing after the war with the nationalization of two other banks and of the 'German Property' (acquired by the German Reich after the annexation of 1938). The latter was taken over by the Allies in 1945 and then returned to Austria as nationalized enterprises, in the Western sectors in 1946/7, and in the Russian sector in 1955 when Austria regained its sovereignty. As a result of these nationalizations a public sector of major importance was created in the Austrian economy; as Ziegler, Reissner and Bender

(1985, p. 75) note:

> Almost 100 per cent of utilities, about two-thirds of mining, iron
> and mineral oil production (measured either by number of people
> employed or by output) is within the public sector. It contributes
> about a quarter to total output of manufacturing industry and
> about 31 per cent to gross domestic product (excluding
> agriculture).

The nationalizations were carried out and maintained by coalition
governments of the People's Party (ÖVP) and the Socialist Party
(SPÖ) which were in power for twenty-one years from the end of
the war; and when one-party government returned in 1966 this did
not change fundamentally the importance of the public sector in the
economy. Since 1970 Austria has had socialist governments –
sometimes in a coalition with the small Freedom Party (FPÖ) and
more recently with the ÖVP again – which have not sought to
extend public ownership by direct nationalization, but have
embarked on economic and social policies inspired by a new
statement of socialist principles that was strongly influenced by
Swedish social democracy: modernization of the industrial
structure, the establishment of a new ministry for health and the
environment (in 1972), reform of the archaic penal code, extension
of the social welfare programme, and a progressive democratization
of society by increasing the participation of workers in the management of industry, improving the dissemination of information, and
encouraging wide-ranging debates on social and political questions.[17]

Sweden and Austria demonstrate how successful a socialistic
society can be in achieving material prosperity, low unemployment
and low inflation (more successful than many other Western
capitalist countries, and very much more successful than Britain),
while at the same time creating greater equality and a substantial
degree of democratic participation in the management of the
economy. Their example has been influential elsewhere in Western
Europe, for instance in France, where frequent references to
Austrian socialism were made by leading members of the French
socialist government of 1981, and also, in a more diffuse way,
wherever socialist governments have been in power, for longer or
shorter periods, since the war.[18] However, in these countries (which

include, besides France, Britain, Norway, the Federal Republic of Germany, Spain and Greece) the periods of socialist government have generally been too short and intermittent, and in some cases their policies have been too limited or ill-prepared, to make possible any substantial advance towards socialism. Britain provides a striking example. The Labour government of 1945 carried out several nationalizations, established a national health service, and expanded the educational system, and to that extent it created conditions favourable to a further advance towards socialism. But it failed lamentably in two major respects: first, it did not bring the leading financial institutions into public ownership, and second, unlike France, it did not create an effective system of central planning. Hence, the socialist project came to a standstill, not even at a 'half-way house' (more like a quarter-way house), and subsequent Labour governments were largely confined to managing the existing system, a weak form of mixed economy in which private capital remained absolutely dominant (aided by Britain's special subordinate relationship with the United States), and to coping as far as possible with its recurrent economic crises.

But there is another great problem confronting the socialistic countries, which arises from the international character of present-day capitalism. Sweden and Austria have been able to pursue their distinctive policies in specific conditions which I have briefly described, and also because, as small economies, they do not present a major threat to international capital. The circumstances are very different when a major European economy begins to move in a socialist direction, as was dramatically illustrated by the difficulties encountered by the French government in 1981, when it tried to overcome the recession by reflating the economy unilaterally. This policy, in the absence of supporting action by other major European economies, produced a balance of payments crisis for France while bringing some benefits in increased trade and production to other countries. As the authors of a study outlining a socialist policy for economic development in Western Europe (Holland 1983) argue, what is needed is a *joint* reflation of the main European economies, with complementary policies of public spending, planning and economic democracy, and public and cooperative enterprise; and since 'the strongest and clearest pressure group against reflation comprises the financial institutions, both official and private . . . methods must be found by which governments can resist the pressure of financial markets' (pp. 63-5).

Establishing effective control at an international level over the financial institutions, through public ownership and other means,[19] evidently presents enormous difficulties, but an advance in this direction could well come in Western Europe as the EC plan for European monetary union is implemented over the next few years; and more particularly because the political influence of socialist and green parties has been steadily growing. The political pressure for a reorientation of European economic and social policies was clearly shown by the results of the European elections in June 1989, and it is reflected in the proposals for a 'social charter' as well as in the movement towards monetary union. This resurgence of what may now perhaps be called 'green socialism' in Western Europe, together with the reforms in Eastern Europe, opens the prospect, in spite of the evident difficulties, of a sustained movement towards a European socialism which would transform the world economy.

But there is still a long way to go, in the first place to catch up with what already exists in Sweden and Austria. In those countries themselves the socialist parties clearly regard their achievements to date as stages in a continuous, gradual process of reform which will lead eventually to a new society. For some socialists, no doubt, the process is all too gradual, and they would prefer more dramatic changes, but I think they are profoundly mistaken in their judgement of the pace at which human attitudes and behaviour are likely to change towards a more cooperative and less competitive mode of life, and also of the real social situation in the advanced capitalist countries in the late twentieth century. Only with the cumulative experience of successful cooperative production and industrial democracy will attitudes slowly change in what Otto Bauer called a 'slow revolution'. As to the social situation, it has to be recognized that for a majority of people in the prosperous capitalist countries it is quite out of the question that they should support or embark upon any sudden and radical transformation of society, especially when they have before their eyes the evidence of its costs in the historical experience of authoritarian socialism.

These issues form the subject matter of the next chapter, the main themes of which can be introduced by bringing together the discussion so far of the problems of socialism in socialist and socialistic countries. In the former, the major reforms that are required – and in many, if not quite all of them, already being implemented – include the extension of democracy, which does not simply mean the introduction of a pluralistic political system, but the creation of something that can best be called a pervasive 'democratic culture'; the decentralization of the economy and changes in the structure of enterprises, not only for the sake of economic efficiency but to promote industrial democracy; and the construction of a new, more sophisticated and indirect system for planning the economy as a whole. In the latter countries, exemplified by Sweden and Austria, the process of continuous reform points to a gradual extension of public ownership, in diverse forms; a growth of public services; and the maintenance and improvement of indirect economic planning.

It is not fanciful to suggest, therefore, that the socialist and the socialistic countries are now slowly converging upon a type of society which would embody the major aspirations of the historical socialist movement in the profoundly changed circumstances of the late twentieth century. Of course, it is customary in the predominantly conservative Western media to interpret the changes now going on in Eastern Europe as some kind of 'return to capitalism', but that is very wide of the mark, at least in most of the countries concerned. For the most part public ownership and central planning are likely to remain, along with the emphasis in their policies on full employment, social welfare and a substantial degree of economic equality; to which may now be added greater democratic participation in all spheres of life. In all these respects they will differ little from the socialistic countries of Western Europe, as the latter continue to pursue their own reforms. What new issues this 'socialism of the future' will have to face has still to be considered after a closer study of the transitional period in which we are presently living.

Notes

1. The term 'socialistic' is intended to refer to those societies, especially in Western Europe, in which socialist or social democratic parties have introduced, at various times since the Second World War, significant elements of a socialist economy, including a substantial amount of public ownership, some degree of central planning, and a general

increase in public expenditure. The experiences of these countries will be discussed later in the text.
2. In Western Europe, particularly, the socialist movement is strong and influential. Thus socialists are by far the largest single group in the European Parliament, and following the European elections in June 1989 they are likely to form a majority in alliance with other left-wing groups, which will have important consequences for the social policies of the EC.
3. Dickinson (1939, p. 9), whom I quoted in an earlier chapter, observed that since the 1920s the term 'planned production' had tended to take the place of 'social ownership' in the definition of socialism and argued that 'there is a close conneksion between these two definitions'. Similarly, Pigou (1937, pp. 6–7) wrote:

> . . .under the influence of the Russian experiment, the definition of general socialism has been modified. Twenty years ago there was little talk of central planning. Socialism entails, it was then held, (1) the extrusion of private profit-making . . . and (2) the public or collective ownership of the means of production (other than human beings). Neither of these requirements singly make necessary any form of central planning; nor do the two together. . . . None the less, at the present day the notion of central planning is commonly introduced into definitions of socialism.

There were, however, indications of the importance of central planning in some earlier Marxist discussions of the future socialist society, notably by Kautsky (1902, pp. 150–1), and more briefly by Hilferding (1910, p. 27) in his reference to a 'consciously regulated' productive community.
4. Hobhouse's study, along with parts of his later work on social justice (Hobhouse 1922), provides one of the most valuable and lucid discussions of the problems of democracy, still highly relevant to the issues facing democratic socialism today.
5. For a critical examination of Hayek's general conception of capitalist society as a spontaneous order, or a 'Great Society', see Bottomore (1985, ch. 4).
6. Even in such a work of Utopian socialism as that of Bellamy, which envisages a large and powerful central administration. William Morris is an exception, but his Utopian novel leaves the economic organization of his ideal society completely vague.
7. Hayek (1982, vol. I, p. 11) writes:

> It is to this philosophical conception [rationalism] that we owe the preference which prevails to the present day for everything that is done 'consciously' and 'deliberately'. . . . Because of this the earlier presumption in favour of traditional or established images became a presumption against them, and 'opinion' came to be thought of as 'mere' opinion – something

not demonstrable or decidable by reason and therefore not to be accepted as a valid ground for decision.

Against this 'constructivist rationalism' he formulates his own conservative philosophy (indistinguishable from that of Edmund Burke) which emphasizes the importance of tradition: 'Many of the institutions of society which are indispensable conditions for the successful pursuit of our conscious aims are in fact the result of customs, habits or practices which have been neither invented nor are observed with any such purpose in view.' And the human being is successful 'because his thinking and acting are governed by rules which have by a process of selection been evolved in the society in which he lives, and which are thus the product of the experience of generations.'

8. In the actual world, economic planning has so far retained its central place, in modified forms, in the socialist countries, and it has acquired an important place in the more successful capitalist economies as well as in such supranational bodies as the EC. So the movement towards a 'rational society' has continued, and the idea of such a society has been vigorously defended against such criticisms as those of Hayek (which indeed have a limited influence), notably by Jürgen Habermas (1971, 1981) who, in his recent work, examines critically the concept of rationality and develops his own conception of the rationalization of the modern world – in a broader sense than that of purely technological rationalization.

9. But Erich Fromm, in some of his later writings, undertook a more thorough analysis of human nature, and particularly of its aggressive and destructive elements (Fromm 1973); and he concluded this last study by saying that he believed it had 'contributed valid arguments in favour of the thesis that aggression and destructiveness can once again assume a minimal role in the fabric of human motivations'.

10. This is the aspect which Heller also emphasizes in her study of Marx's theory of needs (see above, p. 12).

11. Yugoslavia began the process of decentralization much earlier and has moved further along this path, and its central planning system, according to Bornstein (1973, p. 10) can 'best be compared with French-style "indicative" planning'.

12. I use the terms 'public ownership' and 'social ownership' more or less interchangeably. The former is more widely used in the West; the latter perhaps corresponds more closely with the idea of socialism, especially in its 'self-management' form.

13. In this connection the comparison made by Ellman (1989, p. 305) between the German Democratic Republic and the Federal Republic of Germany is instructive:

. . . it appears that labour productivity per *inhabitant* grew faster in the GDR than in the FRG in 1967–76, but per *economically active person* it grew slower in the GDR than in the FRG. (Output growth remained more stable in 1967–76 in the GDR than in the FRG.) This can be interpreted to mean that the inferior performance in dynamic efficiency by the GDR was offset by an increase in the activity rate, i.e. an increase in the burden of work extracted from the population. Alternatively, it can be interpreted to mean that the FRG has an inefficient economic system which wastes much of its potential labour force and deprives many people of the opportunity to participate in paid work.

14. See the discussion of these issues, from diverse points of view, in Duncan (1989).
15. I have discussed the position of the Austrian and Swedish socialist parties in an essay on political trends in Western Europe (Bottomore 1984a, ch. 11).
16. This is discussed more fully in a later essay in the same volume (Ysander 1982).
17. For a more detailed account see Sully (1982, ch. 8).
18. See, for example, the references in Holland (1983, Part 3).
19. See the comment in Holland (1983, p. 66). However, the means of establishing financial control are not very thoroughly examined in the later discussion of new policy priorities.

8

Modes of transition to a socialist economy

The problems of socialism discussed in the previous chapters should not be regarded as unique troubles in an otherwise perfect world, for the problems of capitalism are at least as great, and more fundamental, and so far as they have been contained at all during the post-war period it has been by the adoption of socialistic policies: greatly increased public spending, some extension of public ownership, and more central planning, or in short, the development of various forms of 'mixed economy'. It is the instability of capitalism, characterized by the cycle of boom and slump, its inability to ensure consistent full employment, the gross inequality of wealth and income that it produces, and the impoverished and tawdry culture dominated by money that it creates in its more extreme *laissez-faire* forms, which account for the continued growth of the socialist movement in Western Europe since the war; a growth which has accelerated in recent years as the troubles of capitalism have multiplied. An indication of capitalism's continuing instability was given first by the recession of the late 1970s, then by the stock market crash of October 1987; and some observers expect another, perhaps worse, collapse in the near future, unless it is averted by a profound reform of financial institutions that would involve more public regulation.[1] Meanwhile, unemployment remains high in most of the capitalist countries, and economic growth rates are still low.

In these conditions, the question of a transition to socialism becomes more urgent again, above all in the European societies, and we must begin an examination of this question by outlining the kind of future socialist society to which it is reasonable to aspire. Such a society would be characterized by a substantial degree of public ownership, economic and social planning at a national, regional and local level, and eventually on a transnational scale (as is already the case to a limited but increasing extent); and at the same time a decentralized economy in which the transactions among producers, and between producers and final consumers, would take place in a regulated market system, while the internal structure of enterprises would comprise a large element of self-management. The practice of self-management would indeed be an essential component of socialist democracy, and the latter would be further reinforced by the greater equality of economic and social condition among citizens which it is a primary aim of socialism to establish.

The transition to such a society will necessarily take a different course in Eastern and Western Europe, but there will also be great variations between individual countries, resulting from the diversity of economic and cultural conditions: in the East, the size and strength of different economies, political and cultural traditions, the particular problems of multi-national states; in the West, the existing extent of public ownership, the presence or absence of a planning system, the strength or weakness of individual national economies. In Eastern Europe the two major changes that are needed, and already beginning to be implemented, are the decentralization of the economy and the extension of democracy. The first of these I have discussed in earlier chapters on the experience of socialist planning and on the relation between planning and markets, and I shall return to the subject later in another context with reference to the objectives that should now be formulated by the socialist movement in Western Europe.

The second subject, which I have only briefly referred to earlier in this book, deserves closer attention, particularly in the context of the present debates about political pluralism, the development of new social movements and parties, and the widespread discussion of the scope of democratic participation in economic and social affairs throughout Europe. The socialist movement, from the beginning, stood for an extension of democracy. One of the first major activities of the newly formed socialist parties in the late nineteenth century and early twentieth century was to campaign for universal adult suffrage, which they were largely instrumental in achieving, while at the same time they advocated greater democracy over a wider area – a concern expressed in the name 'social democracy' by which some of them chose to be known. The growth of socialism in Western Europe after the Second World War was checked to a large extent by the unappealing spectacle of the societies of 'real socialism' in Eastern Europe, which remained authoritarian and oppressive even after the death of Stalin, though the active opposition of international capitalism, led by the United States, was also a major factor. Only Yugoslavia offered a more hopeful picture, providing a substantial degree of democratic participation through the self-management system and a relatively liberal political regime, in spite of the absence of opposition parties. The process of democratization which has begun in Eastern Europe is now rapidly changing this situation, and it raises questions, not only about socialist democracy, but also about the future development of democracy in a wider context.

It is misleading to conceive the democratic movement in the socialist countries as simply a belated transformation of these societies into Western-style democracies, with a multi-party system and free elections. Such a conception omits the whole issue of social democracy, and at the same time assumes that democracy in the advanced capitalist countries has attained a state of near perfection beyond which no further advance is possible or desirable. As to the first point, it needs to be strongly asserted that socialist democracy, in its most distinctive form, would be committed to the widest possible participation by citizens in decision-making in all spheres of life. Thus, alongside an electoral system in which various groups and/or parties compete (at national, regional and local levels) on the basis of alternative economic and social policies, there would be institutions ensuring participation in the management of productive enterprises and of educational and cultural organizations. In short, a democratic socialist society would move steadily towards the practical achievement of those ideals formulated in the idea of 'participatory democracy', however long and gradual that process might be.[2] It is a corollary of this view that political power would be less monolithic than it has been until now in the socialist societies, and, as I argued briefly in an earlier chapter, it is quite conceivable that government (at all levels) in the socialist societies of the future would be carried on, during some periods, by coalitions of various groups or parties. Moreover, there should be, and as I conceive it there would be, a considerable devolution of powers from the central government to regional and local governments, while the existence of democratic participation in a multitude of other independent organizations, from enterprises to cultural bodies, would be a further limit on the role of government. This is the manner in which the famous 'withering away of the state' is most likely to be achieved; though today it may be more illuminating to describe it as the socialist version of 'minimum government'.

On the second point, which concerns more particularly the socialist parties in advanced capitalist countries, it should be remembered that democracy, in the sense of universal and equal suffrage, is quite a recent growth in these countries, achieved for the most part only since the First World War, and in some cases after 1945.[3] There is no reason to suppose that the process of democratization will, or should, come to a halt at this point. In the first place there is a need to provide for better representation of the diverse interests and cultural values that exist in a modern society, and this can be met in several ways: by reforming electoral systems to allow for proportional representation (as has been done already in many European countries), and by giving greater powers to regional and local elected assemblies, which are closer to the immediate everyday concerns of citizens. Regrettably, Britain is at present one of the least democratic countries in Western Europe; with a non-elective, totally unrepresentative second chamber, an electoral system which excludes proportional representation and allows a government supported by just over 40 per cent of voters and about one-third of the total electorate to carry out sweeping changes (many of which are opposed by a majority of the population), and a steady erosion of the powers of local government over the past ten years with a corresponding increase in the powers of central government. In the United States the structure of government and the electoral system have similarly, and for a long time, frustrated the development of new parties and consolidated the two-party system, while the electoral process as a whole is dominated, even more than elsewhere, by the power of wealth.

The development of proportional representation in Western Europe is likely to lead, just as in the socialist countries, to political regimes in which coalition governments, representing more faithfully the diversity of values and aims in society but also, I think, increasingly socialistic in their orientation, become more usual, at least for the medium-term future. But this is still not the limit of a democratic transformation of social life, which requires a continued growth of 'social democracy' – the extension of democratic participation to all spheres of life – which is foreshadowed, not only in the current reforms in the socialist countries, but also in the proposals for a 'social charter' that are being discussed in the EC. There are many other aspects of the historical process of democratization, given a new impetus by the reforms in Eastern Europe, that would need to be examined in a comprehensive restatement of the meaning of democracy in the advanced industrial societies of the late twentieth century (among them the institution of more 'open' government and a diminution of the élitism which is partly a survival from earlier forms of society); but I must confine myself here to the brief indications I have already given, and turn now to the mainly economic aspects of a transition to socialism, primarily in the European countries.

In the socialist countries, as I have emphasized, political reform is an essential part of the transition, and it is inextricably interwoven with the economic changes, which require for their success a new spirit of individual enterprise, commitment, and responsibility in production and administration that can only be achieved by enlarging the sphere of free debate, critical judgement and participation in policy-making. The restructuring of management at all levels, from the central ministries to individual enterprises and services, is therefore a crucial feature of the economic reforms. Another fundamental aspect is the development of a coherent and systematic relationship between planning and markets, which is likely to be a gradual and tentative process. As I said earlier, there is no existing theoretical model which can be mechanically applied to solve the problems (although useful indications of possible courses of action are to be found in recent work on the subject);[4] and the balance between market mechanisms and planned development, as well as an effective regulatory system, will have to be discovered largely by experiment and through democratic debate and choice, while drawing upon the experience, both positive and negative, already accumulated in Yugoslavia and Hungary, as well as in some capitalist countries (for example, wartime planning, and the post-war planning in France and Japan).

In the capitalist welfare states of Western Europe, a transition to socialism involves more purely economic changes, and above all an extension of social ownership and planning; but the conditions in which these changes may come about vary greatly from one country to another. In Austria, as we have seen, there is substantial public ownership, and in France the socialist government of 1981 extended public ownership, especially of financial institutions. By contrast, in Britain the privatization mania of the past decade, still continuing, is reducing public ownership to a minimal level, even in essential public services (telephone, gas, electricity, water, railways) which in other European countries are, for the most part, owned and operated by the state (and very efficiently operated, we may add). Any transition to socialism in Britain will, therefore, be long and difficult, the difficulties compounded by the failure ever to create an effective system of central planning; and such progress as there may be is likely to come mainly through the influence of other European countries, and in particular of the EC, in conjunction with the mounting problems of the privatized economy.

But although the problems in Britain are exceptional there are more general questions to be considered about the extension of public ownership. First, let me repeat that public ownership of the major productive resources is essential for the construction of a socialist society; on one side, to eliminate domination by a capitalist class, as a necessary precondition for a broadly 'classless' society, and on the other side, to extend democratic participation as widely as possible, which is simply another aspect of classlessness and equality. In addition, public ownership, including ownership of major financial institutions, is a prerequisite for effective socialist planning. It is evident, however, that conceptions of the scope and nature of public ownership have been changing, and with them the kinds of policy that socialist parties should advocate and can hope to implement in the long term.

It will be useful to begin a discussion of this question by expunging from the socialist vocabulary the term 'nationalization', which now connotes a system in which large centrally administered state corporations dominate the economy. Instead, we should always refer to 'socialization' and 'social ownership', as I have done throughout this book, which may take a variety of forms in accordance with economic circumstances and public policy decisions: state corporations, self-managed enterprises, cooperatives, and perhaps in some spheres mixed private and public undertakings. State corporations are no doubt the most appropriate form in some basic industries and services – airlines, railways, telecommunications, postal services, oil, gas and electricity, engineering, chemicals, car manufacture, and others – but there can well be some regional devolution, and the management of such corporations should always include a large element of self-management by employees, as well as representation of consumer interests. It is not necessary, moreover, that there should be only one state corporation in each sector, and it is indeed desirable that several corporations, competing with each other, should exist in some spheres; for example, in engineering, the car industry, and large-scale retail trade. This point is especially germane to the question of ownership of financial institutions, which is crucial for the development of a socialist economy. The alternative to private ownership is not a single state bank, with ancillary financial services, but a number of socially owned banks and insurance companies, which would, like manufacturers and service industries, compete with each other to some extent; and we must even consider, however shocking this may appear to fundamentalists of one sort or other, the forms which a socialist stock exchange (i.e. a capital market) might take. There is a further issue concerning ownership of productive resources which is of very great importance for the future of socialism, though it has been strangely neglected by socialist parties in recent times: namely, land ownership, which is very unequal in capitalist societies (and particularly so in Britain).[5] The ownership of land is an important element in the wealth and power of the capitalist class, and it is clear that radical changes would be necessary in a socialist society to bring about social ownership. In principle, the land should be regarded as being owned by the community as a whole, but this does not exclude a variety of forms of ownership or possession in practice: medium or long-term leases for agricultural, industrial and commercial purposes; national, municipal and local community ownership of 'common land' for recreational use; individual ownership for dwellings.

The second general form of social ownership, autonomous self-managed enterprises, seems appropriate over a wide range of economic activities, mainly in the field of medium-size producers of goods and services, including much agricultural production, as well as in cultural and leisure activities of all kinds. As I have said, there is much to be learned from the Yugoslav experience, but also from various forms of 'co-determination', which may gradually be extended in Western Europe if the EC 'social charter' is eventually implemented.

In other spheres, and especially in small-scale production and provision of services, cooperative enterprises have an important role to play, and there are indications that the number of cooperatives has been increasing, at a modest rate, in some European countries, sometimes with the help of socialist parties at the national or local level. If in the future, for reasons to be discussed later, there is a growth of small-scale production, then cooperatives will be likely to have a still more important place in the economy. Their particular value is that they are voluntary creations which can be established rapidly (within an appropriate legal framework) to meet new or neglected needs, and of course easily dissolved again if they are not successful. At the same time, individual cooperatives can well form connections with each other, or extend their activities into new fields, thus creating larger cooperative federations which will facilitate and stimulate the overall growth of cooperative production and trade.[6]

But there will also be, in any conceivable socialist society, a relatively large sphere of private production. Exactly how large it will be, and what forms it will take, are questions that cannot be decided in advance, in precise numerical terms, or for the indefinite future. Two considerations are important in this context. The first is that in the advanced industrial countries the number of self-employed persons has tended to increase, along with the expansion of the service sector of the economy, and this trend seems likely to continue.[7] Second, there are benefits to be gained, as I argued earlier, from encouraging small-scale private economic activity in many different fields – in agriculture, artisan production, retail trade, and services – and this may be carried on by self-employed individuals, families, or enterprises employing a small number of workers (though some of the latter could equally well be cooperatives). The persistence, and even expansion, of private economic activity may be seen by some socialists as nurturing an excessive individualism and hence the danger of a rebirth of capitalism; but I think such concerns are exaggerated. Socialism should not be regarded as the antithesis of individualism, but as a specific conception – one which, moreover, has to be continually revised and restated – of the balance to be sought between individual achievement and self-fulfilment, and the attainment of a 'good society', that is to say, a society whose institutions enable *all* individuals, and not simply a privileged minority, to develop as fully as possible their powers of creation and enjoyment. The idea of such a relation between the individual and society is present in all socialist thought, and notably in Marxist thought, although it has sometimes been obscured by an emphasis on the shaping of human nature by impersonal social forces; and some versions of Marxism, as Sartre (1960, p. 58) observed, had 'completely lost the sense of what a human being is'.

It is true that private production does not socialize individuals in the production process, does not incorporate them into the body of 'associated producers' in any direct manner, but they would still participate in the cooperative life of a socialist community in many other ways, through their relations with the sphere of socialized production and public services, and their involvement in numerous processes of democratic decision-making in public affairs. In any event, the sphere of socialized production, in the form of state corporations, self-managed enterprises, and cooperatives, would have a predominant place in the economy, accounting perhaps for at least half of all manufacture, a substantial part of agriculture and trade, and a very large part of the provision of basic services such as health, education, transport and general public utilities; and there would be social ownership or effective control of land and financial institutions.

But the movement towards the kind of society I have sketched here is bound to be gradual, and very uneven between countries, in the economic conditions of the late twentieth century. Sidney Webb's argument that 'important organic changes can only be democratic . . . acceptable to a majority of the people . . . prepared for in the minds of all . . . gradual, and thus causing no dislocation' (see above, p. 14) is now much more apposite than when it was first propounded. In Britain, after the wholesale privatizations, the extension of public ownership and central planning will be exceptionally difficult; but in Western Europe generally,[8] even in more favourable circumstances, it seems unlikely that the old-style method of buying out the shareholders in private industry will play a major part in the process of socialization, although it can still be used effectively in some cases, particularly where capitalist enterprises run into economic difficulties during a recession, or where public opinion turns strongly against private monopolies.

In any case, there are alternative methods, among them the Swedish project for collective capital formation through employee or wage-earner investment funds, which emerged from discussions at the 1971 Congress of the Swedish Confederation of Trade Unions (LO) and the resulting detailed study by Meidner (1978). Briefly, Meidner's original scheme proposed a method of accumulating 'collective capital' by a levy on the pre-tax profits of companies employing more than fifty workers, the proceeds of which would be paid into a central fund in the form of newly issued shares. The capital accumulated in this way, and by the purchase of additional shares out of the income on shareholdings, would eventually give employees a substantial holding in the companies, leading to the nomination of board members in individual companies and a more general control through the administration of this collective capital by regional or sectoral funds (Meidner 1978, ch. 7). Over a period of twenty-five to sixty years, depending on the profitability of companies, a large part of the Swedish economy would in this way be socialized (Olsen 1989, ch. 2). As a result of subsequent discussions and studies, however, Meidner's plan was considerably modified, and the legislation introduced in 1983 established a much less radical scheme, which applied only to large companies (with 500 or more employees), involved a tax only on 'excess profits' plus a payroll tax, accumulated funds in cash instead of shares, created regional rather than sectoral funds (though with a majority of employees on their boards), and changed the main emphasis of the plan from socialization and workers' control to the accumulation of investment capital (Olsen 1989, ch. 2). The scheme was also introduced explicitly as an experiment for a limited period, to be reviewed in 1990, and it seems now to be the intention not to continue it beyond that date, by which time the funds will have only about 8 per cent of the 1983 value of shares quoted on the Stockholm stock exchange (Olsen 1989, ch. 2). Nevertheless, the review of the 'experiment' may itself generate new interest in the scheme and revive the debate about alternative methods of socializing the economy; and it will provide valuable lessons for other socialist parties and governments throughout Europe.

Among other methods of extending social ownership we should consider, particularly, increased support for small-scale cooperative production, which can be provided very effectively at the municipal or local level, and the creation of new enterprises where this is necessary, especially in the financial sphere. For example, in Britain, where none of the commercial banks, or other major financial institutions, were ever taken into public ownership, a significant beginning might be made in extending social ownership by the establishment of new banks, particularly an investment bank and perhaps also some community banks, and at the same time applying to the existing privately owned banks some appropriate version of the employee investment funds scheme.[9] In other countries of Western Europe, where there is more extensive social ownership of financial institutions, of major infrastructural services, and to some extent of manufacturing industry, the development of a socialist economy will be relatively easier. The influence of these countries, together with that of the reformed socialist societies of Eastern Europe, is likely to be a major factor in the evolution of Europe as a whole over the next few decades. What is evident, indeed, is that the transition to socialism has become, more than it ever was in the past, a supranational process, and there is a corresponding need for socialist thinkers and politicians to work out programmes, policies and mechanisms, on a European basis, for advancing from welfare capitalism and 'socialistic' regimes towards a more distinctively socialist economy. There is an example of such collaboration in the report by Holland (1983), although this was a project for European recovery rather than specifically for European socialism.

Many such projects, with a socialist orientation, should now be initiated in order to prepare for the new opportunities that will emerge in the next decade. If socialist (or socialist/green) parties come to power in several more European countries, and if the restructuring of the socialist economies in Eastern Europe begins to produce successful results, then a decisive movement towards socialism will be possible, and for this to continue and endure there must be carefully prepared and coordinated action by socialist governments, drawing upon the experience of all of them in developing forms of social ownership, with a strong emphasis upon self-management, and in creating efficacious types of central planning. Not only the achievement, but the satisfactory operation of a socialist economy is, and will remain, a complex and difficult task, and we must hope that the present and future generations will in fact display that degree of intelligence in coping with it which Engels confidently anticipated.

The task is all the more complex and daunting because socialist governments must try to achieve, over a period of time, a number of different aims which are not easily reconciled and coordinated. First, they have to maintain the comfortable standards of living which can now be regarded as customary for a majority of the population in the developed industrial countries, while at the same time extending such conditions of life to the still considerable numbers of those in poverty, and reducing the wealth of a small privileged minority. Maintaining these standards will, however, depend increasingly upon public rather than private provision for many basic needs, and a socialist government will not necessarily be committed to unlimited aggregate economic growth regardless of what is growing and what social and environmental costs it entails. The emphasis in all socialist policies should be on improving the quality of life for the whole population, not on sheer economic growth, and it is to be hoped that a time will come when the achievements of different countries will be judged in terms of the former criterion, rather than by their relative position in some international league of growth rates.

This question is especially relevant in considering a second concern of socialist governments: namely, how they can best contribute to overcoming poverty in the poorer countries of the Third World, where economic development is undoubtedly needed. It is evident to all that the present division of the world between wealthy and poor countries cannot, and should not, continue indefinitely. But there are two aspects of this situation to be considered. In the first place, what are the policies and mechanisms that can most effectively help the poor countries? There is a great deal of accumulated experience of successful, and unsuccessful, aid to these countries, in which both the objectives of donor nations and the character of the indigenous regimes are important factors, but I do not think that there has yet emerged a distinctive and coordinated socialist policy to overcome international economic inequalities; or second, a serious and thorough consideration of the consequences of economic development on a global scale and their implications for the industrial countries themselves. Let us suppose that over the next half-century many of the poor countries, with the help of socialist industrial nations, succeed in raising the standard of living of their populations substantially, and that the middle-income countries of the Third World continue effectively their policies of industrialization and general economic development, so that they begin to catch up with the advanced industrial societies. It is evident – and we can picture the situation most vividly by imagining that every country in the world eventually attained living standards equal to those in the prosperous West European societies – that economic development on this scale, coupled with population growth, would place an enormous burden on the earth's resources, in land, energy, food and minerals, and would add massively to the problems of pollution and damage to the earth's atmosphere.[10] So there is an obvious need, in considering the longer term, for a great deal more planning, with an international scope, based on policies which would tackle simultaneously the overcoming of poverty in the Third World, limiting the growth of population, and restricting or eliminating non-sustainable and damaging types of economic growth.[11]

Many socialist parties, I think, have not yet seriously confronted such issues, and for that reason there has been a rapid increase in the support for green parties which propose more definite and radical policies; though the eventual outcome may be, as I suggested earlier and as I hope, the emergence of a new, 'green socialism'. In fact, most of the questions that I have raised concerning the present-day problems of socialism and possible modes of transition to a socialist economy point in that direction. The decentralization of economic decision-making through the development of self-managed enterprises, cooperatives and individual self-employment, would encourage in various ways the growth of smaller, more local productive enterprises; and even though some enterprises must necessarily be organized on a large scale – railways, car manufacture, some engineering and chemical plants – there is no reason why large enterprises themselves should be brought together in giant corporations, whether private or public. The recent wave of mergers and takeovers in the capitalist world has been dictated more by financial speculation, boundless profit-seeking, and the desire to eliminate competition, than by any very obvious economic need, or benefit to the population at large.[12]

The development of small-scale production and provision of

services, wherever this is feasible, would, on the contrary, bring considerable social and environmental benefits. Socially, it would enlarge the sphere in which individuals can have some real control over their working lives and participate effectively in decision-making. Environmentally, in conjunction with the greater powers of local government, it would be likely to increase concern for the natural surroundings in which people live and work, and to reduce the congestion resulting from long journeys to work. The shape of an alternative economy for the twenty-first century is now unmistakably beginning to appear, at least in very broad outline, and socialist projects for the near future as well as for the longer term of the next half-century should take account of the new possibilities and the new public attitudes that are emerging.

Any transition to socialism will require extensive and flexible planning, of an indirect, indicative kind, if the diverse aims I have sketched here – greater equality of wealth and income in each country and in the world as a whole, more extensive public ownership and democratic participation in all the affairs of social life, and a reorientation of economic development to accord with these aims and also with the protection and renewal of the human habitat – are to be achieved, however gradually. There is one aspect of planning which should be particularly stressed; namely, the need to take account, in constructing social and economic plans, not only of the market prices or 'accounting prices' derived from them, of all the elements – material resources and labour – which constitute the 'productive forces', but also of the ways of valuing the exhaustible resources which can be allocated between generations. The subject is discussed in some detail in a study of the history of 'ecological economics' by Martinez-Alier (1987), who considers some of its implications for development policies in the Third World and also in the wealthy industrial countries, where zero growth, or low and selective growth, may be desirable in the future.

These questions are of great importance for socialists, but they have received little attention until very recently. One of these who considered them at an earlier time was Otto Neurath, who specifically raised in his discussion of a 'natural economy' the issue of valuing, and making a choice between, the present and future use of non-renewable resources (see p. 21 above). Neurath also advocated, as an integral part of socialist planning which would take account of physical resources (materials and energy), the construction of alternative 'scientific Utopias' which would be an essential element in a continuous process of social transformation, and this idea too is valuable for the present generation of socialists. The strength and success of the socialist movement came historically from its vision of a completely new society, but today that vision seems to have faded, and socialism in many countries, lacking an intellectual content (as distinct from various kinds of technical expertise), is orientated, for the most part, to the achievement of modest reforms. A cautious and uninspired pragmatism has almost vanquished Utopianism. Yet without the latter I do not think there can be any movement deserving to be called socialist or capable of engendering the enthusiasm and political will necessary to bring about substantial social change. Not Utopianism in the sense of a belief that human society and human nature can be miraculously transformed overnight in order to remedy all the multiple problems and injustices of the existing world, but as the forceful statement of an ideal to be attained over a long period, by the variety of means that I have discussed, and through the successive elaboration of, and widespread debate about, what we may call 'interim Utopias'.

The transition I have sketched here is not located in some distant future. On the contrary, it began early in this century in a diversity of forms, and since the end of the Second World War has passed through major phases of success and failure which are briefly charted in this book. From that experience there have emerged the new movements and new ideas of recent years which have still to be clearly recognized in a statement of socialist aims and policies – a new socialist manifesto – that would bring together the ideal of a socialist society and the sequence of practical measures through which it can be approached, in the manner and at the tempo considered desirable by a majority of the population. It is above all in Europe, East and West, that the circumstances are now most favourable for such a venture.

Notes

1. The French economist Maurice Allais, for example, in an article in *Le Monde* (26 June 1989) anticipates a new period of turbulence, and

observes that economic instability, social injustice, and poverty are the bane of market economies.

2. I have discussed the diverse conceptions of democracy more fully in Bottomore (1979, ch. 1). See also the discussion of the relation between democratic ideas and élite theories in Albertoni (1987, Part II).

3. See Bottomore (1979, ch. 1).

4. For example, in Horvat (1982, ch. 12) and Selucky (1979).

5. See the data in Scott (1982), in particular his estimate that 'about 200 peerage families holding estates of 5,000 acres or more owned about one-third of the British land area', and his summary of research by McEwan (1977) on 'the phenomenally high percentage of landowners among Britain's wealthy élite' (p. 103), even in recent times.

6. A good example of this process is the Mondragon cooperative in Spain which has grown from small beginnings into a fairly large and successful association of cooperatives (Thomas and Logan 1982).

7. This is very evident in Britain and also in some socialist countries, for example in Hungary's 'second economy'.

8. In the following discussion I exclude from consideration the United States, where the possibility of socialism seems to belong to a very remote future. Hence there will be for a long time, on any reasonable reckoning, two economic systems – capitalist and socialist – coexisting in the world and influencing in different ways the development of the poorer countries of the Third World.

9. See the discussion in Coakley and Harris (1983, ch. 10) of the need to 'nationalize' the major financial institutions and, just as important, to change the character of their operations (which does not always necessarily follow the change of ownership, as the experience of the nationalizations by the socialist government in France in 1982 indicates). The authors do not, however, suggest any definite procedures by which social ownership and a change in the orientation of financial policies could actually be achieved in the existing social and political conditions, and conclude only in very general terms that preparation has to be made to overcome the difficulties that socialization presents.

10. See the discussion, with particular reference to population growth, in Faaland (1982).

11. Much has been written on this subject since the publication of the pessimistic projections of the Club of Rome (Meadows *et al.*, 1972), including discussions of the 'social limits to growth' (Hirsch 1977); and the rapid development of environmentalist movements and green parties in the 1980s is an indication that economic policy-making has entered a period of profound change.

12. In one sphere, particularly, the effects of 'gigantism' are very clear. There is no value at all (except financial gain for a small number of

people) in the emergence of giant publishing corporations, controlling a wide range of newspapers, magazines, book publishing, television and radio stations; and we should all be a great deal better off, in terms of literacy and the general level of culture, if such activities were carried on by a large number of independent medium-size enterprises.

Bibliography

Albertoni, Ettore A. (1987) *Mosca and the Theory of Elitism*, Oxford: Blackwell.

Aron, Raymond (1960) 'Social class, political class, ruling class', reprinted in Aron (1988).

Aron, Raymond (1965) 'Ruling groups or ruling class?', reprinted in Aron (1988).

Aron, Raymond (1968) *Democracy and Totalitarianism*, London: Weidenfeld & Nicolson.

Aron, Raymond (1988) *Power, Modernity and Sociology*, Aldershot: Edward Elgar.

Bahro, Rudolf (1982) *Socialism and Survival*, London: Heretic Books.

Bauer, Otto (1923) *Die Österreichische Revolution*, Vienna: Wiener Volksbuchhandlung; abridged English version, New York: Burt Franklin, 1925.

Bauer, Otto (1931) *Kapitalismus und Sozialismus nach dem Weltkrieg*, vol. I, *Rationalisierung oder Fehlrationalisierung?* Vienna: Wiener Volksbuchhandlung.

Bellamy, Edward (1887) *Looking Backward*, New York: The Modern Library, 1951.

Berliner, Joseph S. (1988) *Soviet Industry from Stalin to Gorbachev*, Aldershot: Edward Elgar.

Bernstein, Eduard (1899) *Evolutionary Socialism*, New York: Schocken, 1961.

Bjerve, Petter J. (1959) *Planning in Norway: 1947–1956*, Amsterdam: North-Holland.

Bornstein, Morris (ed.) (1973) *Plan and Market: Economic Reform in*

Eastern Europe, New Haven: Yale University Press.

Bornstein, Morris (ed.) (1975) *Economic Planning, East and West*, Cambridge, Mass.: Bellinger.

Bottomore, Tom (1964) *Elites and Society*, Harmondsworth: Penguin Books, 1966.

Bottomore, Tom (1975) *Sociology as Social Criticism*, London: Allen & Unwin.

Bottomore, Tom (1979) *Political Sociology*, London: Hutchinson.

Bottomore, Tom (ed.) (1983) *A Dictionary of Marxist Thought*, Oxford: Blackwell.

Bottomore, Tom (1984a) *Sociology and Socialism*, Brighton: Wheatsheaf.

Bottomore, Tom (1984b) *The Frankfurt School*, Chichester/London: Ellis Horwood/Tavistock.

Bottomore, Tom (1985) *Theories of Modern Capitalism*, London: Allen & Unwin.

Bottomore, Tom (1986–7) 'Is rivalry rational?', *Critical Review*, Winter.

Bottomore, Tom (ed.) (1988) *Interpretations of Marx*, Oxford: Blackwell).

Bottomore, Tom and Robert J. Brym (eds) (1989) *The Capitalist Class: An International Study*, Hemel Hempstead: Harvester-Wheatsheaf.

Bricianer, Serge (1978) *Pannekoek and the Workers' Councils*, St. Louis, Missouri: Telos.

Britain Without Capitalists: A Study of What Industry in a Soviet Britain Could Achieve (1936) by a group of economists, scientists and technicians, London: Lawrence & Wishart.

Broekmeyer, M. J. (ed.) (1970) *Yugoslav Workers' Self-management*, Dordrecht: Reidel.

Brubaker, Rogers (1984) *The Limits of Rationality: An Essay on the Social and Moral Thought of Max Weber*, London: Allen & Unwin.

Buck, Trevor and John Cole (1987) *Modern Soviet Economic Performance*, Oxford: Blackwell.

Bukharin, Nikolai (1920) *Economics of the Transformation Period*, New York: Bergman, 1971).

Carr, E. H. (1952) *A History of Soviet Russia: The Bolshevik Revolution 1917–1923*, vol. 2., London: Macmillan.

Chossudovsky, Michel (1986) *Towards Capitalist Restoration? Chinese Socialism after Mao*, London: Macmillan.

Coakley, Jerry and Laurence Harris (1983) *The City of Capital*, Oxford: Blackwell.

Cole, G. D. H. (1920) *Guild Socialism Re-stated*, London: Parsons.

Cole, G. D. H. (1954) *A History of Socialist Thought*, vol. II, *Marxism and Anarchism, 1850–1890*, London: Macmillan.

Devons, Ely (1970) *Papers on Planning and Economic Management*, Manchester: University of Manchester Press.

Dickinson, H. D. (1939) *Economics of Socialism*, London: Oxford University Press.

Djilas, Milovan (1957) *The New Class*, London: Thames & Hudson.

Dobb, Maurice (1928) *Russian Economic Development since the Revolution*, London: Routledge; 2nd edn 1929.

Dore, Ronald (1987) *Taking Japan Seriously*, London: Athlone Press.

Duncan, Graeme (ed.) (1989) *Democracy and the Capitalist State*, Cambridge: Cambridge University Press.

Durbin, E. F. M. (1949) *Problems of Economic Planning*, London: Routledge & Kegan Paul.

Ellman, Michael (1989) *Socialist Planning*, 2nd edn, Cambridge: Cambridge University Press.

Engels, Friedrich (1881) 'Letter to Karl Kautsky, 1 February'.

Engels, Friedrich (1894) Foreword to *Internationales aus dem 'Volksstaat' (1871-75)*.

Erlich, Alexander (1960) *The Soviet Industrialization Debate, 1924-1928*, Cambridge, Mass.: Harvard University Press.

Faaland, Just (ed.) (1982) *Population and the World Economy in the 21st Century*, Oxford: Blackwell.

Ferge, Zsuzsa (1979) *A Society in the Making: Hungarian Social and Societal Policy, 1945-75*, Harmondsworth: Penguin Books.

Fourastié, Jean and Jean-Paul Courthéoux, (1963) *La planification économique en France*, Paris: Presses Universitaires de France.

Fromm, Erich (1973) *The Anatomy of Human Destructiveness*, New York: Holt, Rinehart and Winston.

Gabor, Dennis (1970) *Innovations: Scientific, Technological and Social*, London: Oxford University Press.

Gábor, I. and P. Galasi (1981) 'The labour market in Hungary since 1968', in Hare, Radice and Swain (eds) (1981).

Gay, Peter (1952) *The Dilemma of Democratic Socialism: Eduard Bernstein's Challenge to Marx*, New York: Columbia University Press.

George, Vic and Nick Manning (1980) *Socialism, Social Welfare and the Soviet Union*, London: Routledge & Kegan Paul.

Glass, S. T. (1966) *The Responsible Society: The Ideas of Guild Socialism*, London: Longmans, Green.

Golubović, Zagorka (1986) 'Yugoslav society and "socialism" ', in Golubović and Stojanovic', *The Crisis of the Yugoslav System*, Study no. 14 in the Research Project 'Crises in Soviet-type systems', Cologne: Index.

Gramsci, Antonio (1919-20) 'Soviets in Italy', *New Left Review*, 51, Sept./ Oct., 1968.

Granick, D. (1975) *Enterprise Guidance in Eastern Europe*, Princeton: Princeton University Press.

Gulick, Charles A. (1948) *Austria from Habsburg to Hitler* (2 vols), Berkeley and Los Angeles: University of California Press.

Habermas, Jürgen (1971) *Toward a Rational Society*, London: Heinemann.

Habermas, Jürgen (1976) *Legitimation Crisis*, London: Heinemann.

Habermas, Jürgen (1981) *The Theory of Communicative Action* (2 vols), Boston: Beacon Press, 1984, 1987.

Hardach, Gerd and Dieter Karras (1978) *A Short History of Socialist Economic Thought*, London: Edward Arnold.

Hare, Paul, Hugo Radice, and Nigel Swain, (1981) *Hungary: A Decade of Economic Reform*, London: Allen & Unwin.

Hayek, F. A. (ed.) (1935) *Collectivist Economic Planning: Critical Studies on the Possibilities of Socialism*, London: Routledge.

Hayek, F. A. (1944) *The Road to Serfdom*, London: Routledge.

Hayek, F. A. (1948) *Individualism and Economic Order*, Chicago: University of Chicago Press.

Hayek, F.A. (1982) *Law, Legislation and Liberty* (3 vols in 1), London: Routledge & Kegan Paul.

Hegedüs, András (1976) *Socialism and Bureaucracy*, London: Allison & Busby.

Heller, Agnes (1976) *The Theory of Need in Marx*, London: Allison & Busby.

Hilferding, Rudolf (1910) *Finance Capital: A Study of the Latest Phase of Capitalist Development*, London: Routledge & Kegan Paul, 1981.

Hilferding, Rudolf (1927) 'Die Aufgaben der Sozialdemokratie in der Republik' (published speech, Berlin).

Hilferding, Rudolf (1940) 'State capitalism or totalitarian state economy', *Socialist Courier*, New York, reprinted in *Modern Review*, New York, I, (1947).

Hilferding, Rudolf (1941) 'Das historische Problem', unfinished manuscript first published, edited and introduced by Benedikt Kautsky, in *Zeitschrift für Politik* (New Series), I, 1954.

Hindess, Barry (1989) *Reactions to the Right*, London: Routledge.

Hirsch, Fred (1977) *Social Limits to Growth*, London: Routledge & Kegan Paul.

Hobhouse, L. T. (1918) *The Metaphysical Theory of the State*, London: Allen & Unwin.

Hobhouse, L. T. (1922) *The Elements of Social Justice*, London: Allen & Unwin.

Holland, Stuart (ed.) (1983) *Out of Crisis: A Project for European Recovery*, Nottingham: Spokesman.

Horvat, Branko (1982) *The Political Economy of Socialism*, Oxford: Martin Robertson.

Hutchison, T. W. (1981) *The Politics and Philosophy of Economics: Marxians, Keynesians and Austrians*, Oxford: Blackwell.

Jacobs, Paul and Saul Landau (eds) (1966) *The New Radicals: A Report With Documents*, New York: Random House.

Jászi, Oscar (1934) 'Socialism', in *Encyclopaedia of the Social Sciences*, vol. 14, New York: Macmillan.

Jessop, Bob (1982) *The Capitalist State*, Oxford: Martin Robertson.

Kaser, M. C. (ed.) (1986) *The Economic History of Eastern Europe*, vol. 3, *Institutional Change within a Planned Economy*, Oxford: Clarendon Press.

Kautsky, Karl (1902) *The Social Revolution*, Chicago: Charles H. Kerr.

Kolakowski, Leszek and Stuart Hampshire (eds) (1974) *The Socialist Idea: A Reappraisal*, London: Weidenfeld & Nicolson.

Komiya, Ryutaro (1975) 'Planning in Japan', in Bornstein (ed.), *Economic Planning, East and West*.

Konrád, G. and Szelényi, I. (1979) *The Intellectuals on the Road to Class Power*, Brighton: Harvester.

Kowalik, Tadeusz (1987a) 'Lange, Oskar Ryszard', in *The New Palgrave: A Dictionary of Economics*, vol. 3, London: Macmillan.

Kowalik, Tadeusz (1987b) 'Lange-Lerner mechanism', in *The New Palgrave: A Dictionary of Economics*, vol. 3, London: Macmillan.

Landauer, Carl (1959) *European Socialism: A History of Ideas and Movements from the Industrial Revolution to Hitler's Seizure of Power*, 2 vols, Berkeley and Los Angeles: University of California Press.

Lange, O. and Taylor, F. M. (1938) *On the Economic Theory of Socialism*, Minneapolis: University of Minnesota Press.

Larrain, Jorge (1986) *A Reconstruction of Historical Materialism*, London: Allen & Unwin.

Lavoie, Don (1985) *Rivalry and Central Planning*, Cambridge: Cambridge University Press.

Leiss, W. (1972) *The Domination of Nature*, New York: Braziller.

Löwith, Karl (1932) *Max Weber and Karl Marx*, London: Allen & Unwin, 1982.

Marcuse, Herbert (1964) *One-Dimensional Man*, Boston: Beacon Press.

Marković, Mihailo (1983) 'Human nature', in Bottomore (ed.) (1983).

Marschak, Thomas A. (1973) 'Decentralizing the command economy: the study of a pragmatic strategy for reformers', in Bornstein (ed.) (1973).

Martinez-Alier, Juan (1987) *Ecological Economics*, Oxford: Blackwell.

Marx, Karl and Friedrich Engels (1845-6) *The German Ideology*.

Marx, Karl and Friedrich Engels (1848) *Communist Manifesto*.

Marx, Karl (1857-8) *Grundrisse: Foundations of the Critique of Political Economy (Rough Draft)*, Harmondsworth: Penguin Books in association with *New Left Review*, 1973.

Marx, Karl (1894) *Capital*, vol. III.

McEwan, J. (1977) *Who Owns Scotland?*, Edinburgh: EUSPB.

Meadows, Donella H., Dennis L. Meadows, Jørgen Randers and William W. Behrens, (1972) *The Limits to Growth: A Report for the Club of Rome's Project on the Predicament of Mankind*, New York: Signet.

Meidner, Rudolf (1978) *Employee Investment Funds: An Approach to Collective Capital Formation*, London: Allen & Unwin.

Michels, R. (1911) *Political Parties*, New York: The Free Press, 1966.

Mises, Ludwig von (1920) 'Economic calculation in the socialist commonwealth', in Hayek (1935), pp. 87–103.

Mises, Ludwig von (1922) *Socialism: An Economic and Sociological Analysis*, London: Jonathan Cape, 1936.

Montias, J. M. (1968) 'Planning, Economic (Eastern Europe)', in *International Encyclopaedia of the Social Sciences*, vol. 12, New York: Macmillan and The Free Press.

Moore, Stanley (1980) *Marx on the Choice between Socialism and Communism*, Cambridge, Mass.: Harvard University Press.

Morioka, Koji (1989) 'Japan', in Bottomore and Brym (eds), *The Capitalist Class*.

Morris, William (1890) *News from Nowhere*, London: Longmans, Green, 1914.

Morris, William (1907) *A Factory As It Might Be*, London: Twentieth Century Press.

Myrdal, Gunnar (1960) *Beyond the Welfare State*, London: Duckworth.

Nettl, J. P. (1965) 'The German Social Democratic Party 1890–1914 as a political model', *Past and Present*, vol. 30.

Neurath, Otto (1919) *Through the War Economy to the Natural Economy*, in English in Neurath (1973).

Neurath, Otto (1920) Lecture on experiences of socialization in Bavaria, in Neurath (1973), pp. 18–28.

Neurath, Otto (1928) *Personal Life and Class Struggle*, in Neurath (1973).

Neurath, Otto (1973) *Empiricism and Sociology*, edited by Marie Neurath and Robert S. Cohen, Dordrecht: Reidel.

Nove, Alec (1964) *Was Stalin Really Necessary?*, London: Allen & Unwin.

Nove, Alec (1969) *An Economic History of the USSR*, London: Allen Lane.

Nove, Alec (1983) *The Economics of Feasible Socialism*, London: Allen & Unwin.

Nuti, Domenico Mario (1988) 'Perestroika: transition from central planning to market socialism', *Economic Policy*, 7.

Olsen, Gregg (1989) *On the Limits of Social Democracy: The Rise and Fall of the Swedish Wage Earner Funds*, unpublished PhD dissertation, Toronto.

Pigou, A. C. (1937) *Socialism versus Capitalism*, London: Macmillan, 1960.

Pollock, Friedrich (1929) *Die planwirtschaftlichen Versuche in der Sowjetunion 1917–1927*, Frankfurt: Verlag Neue Kritik, 1971.

Porter, Cathy (1980) *Alexandra Kollontai: A Biography*, London: Virago.

Postan, M. M. (1967) *Economic History of Western Europe, 1945–64*, London: Methuen.

Preobrazhensky, Evgeny (1926) *The New Economics*, Oxford: Oxford University Press, 1965.

Pribićević, Branko (1959) *The Shop Stewards' Movement and Workers' Control, 1910–1922*, Oxford: Blackwell.

Renner, Karl (1916) 'Probleme des Marxismus', *Der Kampf*, IX.

Renner, Karl (1921) 'Demokratie und Rätesystem', *Der Kampf*, XIV, 54–67.

Richet, X. (1981) 'Is there an "Hungarian" model of planning?', in Hare, Radice and Swain (eds) (1981).

Richta, Radovan *et al.* (1969) *Civilization at the Crossroads*, White Plains, NY: International Arts and Science Press.

Robbins, Lionel (1934) *The Great Depression*, London: Macmillan.

Rydén, Bengt and Villy Bergström (eds) (1982) *Sweden: Choices for Economic and Social Policy in the 1980s*, London: Allen & Unwin.

Sartre, Jean-Paul (1960) *Critique of Dialectical Reason*, London: New Left Books, 1976.

Schumpeter, J. A. (1908) *Das Wesen und der Hauptinhalt der theoretischen Nationalökonomie*, Munich and Leipzig: Duncker & Humblet.

Schumpeter, J. A. (1939) *Business Cycles: A Theoretical, Historical and Statistical Analysis of the Capitalist Process*, New York: McGraw-Hill.

Schumpeter, J. A. (1942) *Capitalism, Socialism and Democracy*, 6th edn, London: Allen & Unwin, 1987.

Schumpeter, J.A. (1954) *History of Economic Analysis*, London: Allen & Unwin.

Scientific-Technological Revolution: Social Aspects (1977), papers presented at the Eighth World Congress of the International Sociological Association, London: Sage.

Scott, J. (1982) *The Upper Classes: Property and Privilege in Britain*, London: Macmillan.

Seibel, Claude (1975) 'Planning in France', in Bornstein (ed.), *Economic Planning, East and West*.

Selucký, Radoslav (1979) *Marxism, Socialism, Freedom: Towards a General Democratic Theory of Labour-Managed Systems*, London, Macmillan.

Shaw, G. Bernard (1931) *Fabian Essays in Socialism*, London: The Fabian Society and Allen & Unwin.

Singleton, Fred (1985) *A Short History of the Yugoslav Peoples*, Cambridge: Cambridge University Press.

Springborg, Patricia (1981) *The Problem of Human Needs and the Critique of Civilisation*, London: Allen & Unwin.

Spulber, Nicolas (ed.) (1964) *Foundations of Soviet Strategy for Economic Growth: Selected Soviet Essays, 1924–1930*, Bloomington: Indiana University Press.

Stalin, J. V. (1955) *Works*, vol. 13, Moscow: Foreign Languages Publishing House.

Stojanović, Svetozar (1973) *Between Ideals and Reality: A Critique of Socialism and its Future*, New York: Oxford University Press.

Stokman, F. N., R. Ziegler and J. Scott (eds) (1985) *Networks of Corporate Power*, Cambridge: Polity Press.

Sully, Melanie A. (1982) *Continuity and Change in Austrian Socialism: The Eternal Quest for the Third Way*, Boulder: East European Monographs, distributed by Columbia University Press.

Sweezy, Paul (ed.) (1949) *Böhm-Bawerk: Karl Marx and the Close of his System*, New York: Augustus M. Kelley.

Széll, György (1988) 'Participation, workers' control and self-management', *Current Sociology*, 36 (3).

Thomas, Hank and Logan, Chris (1982) *Mondragon: An Economic Analysis*, London: Allen & Unwin.

Tinbergen, J. (1968) 'Planning, Economic (Western Europe)', in *International Encyclopaedia of the Social Sciences*, vol. 12, New York: Macmillan and The Free Press.

Van der Pijl, Kees (1989) 'The International Level', in Bottomore and Brym (eds) (1989).

Webb, Sidney and Beatrice (1935) *Soviet Communism: A New Civilisation?* London: Longmans, Green.

Weber, Max (1918) 'Socialism', English trans. in J. E. T. Eldridge (ed.), *Max Weber: The Interpretation of Social Reality*, London: Michael Joseph, 1970.

White, Gordon, Robin Murray and Christine White (eds) (1983) *Revolutionary Socialist Development in the Third World*, Brighton: Wheatsheaf.

Wicksteed, P. H. (1933) *The Common Sense of Political Economy*, 2nd edn, 2 vols, London: Routledge & Kegan Paul.

Wilczynski, J. (1982) *The Economics of Socialism*, 4th edn, London: Allen & Unwin.

Wirth, Margaret (1972) *Kapitalismustheorie in der DDR: Entstehung und Entwicklung der Theorie des staatsmonopolistischen Kapitalismus*, Frankfurt: Suhrkamp.

Wootton, Barbara (1934) *Plan or No Plan*, London: Gollancz.

Yeo, Stephen (1987) 'Three socialisms: statism, collectivism, associationism', in William Outhwaite and Michael Mulkay (eds), *Social Theory and Social Criticism*, Oxford: Blackwell.

Ysander, Bengt-Christer (1982) 'Income formation in a mixed economy', in Rydén and Bergström (eds) (1982).

Ziegler, Rolf, Gerhard Reissner and Donald Bender (1985) 'Austria incorporated', in Stokman, Ziegler and Scott (eds) (1985).

Index

accumulation, 29
agriculture, 17, 42, 64, 94-5
Aron, Raymond, 61, 63
Austria, 39, 113-14, 126
Austro-Marxism, 27

base and superstructure, 2
Bauer, Otto, 27, 116
Bavarian Soviet, 24, 36
Bellamy, Edward, 10, 17, 19, 84, 104
Bender, Donald, 113
Bergström, Villy, 112
Berliner, Joseph S., 65, 73, 74, 75
Bernstein, Eduard, 13, 14
Besant, Annie, 14, 15
Böhm-Bawerk, Eugen, 52-3
Britain, 19, 39, 41, 45-6, 48, 72, 79,
    112, 114, 115, 124, 126, 129, 131
Bukharin, Nikolai, 28-9, 34, 35
bureaucracy, 57, 60-2, 73-5, 104

capitalism, 19, 36, 45-8, 66-7, 80, 121
China, 43, 93-4
civil society, 73, 97
class, 13, 35
Cole, G. D. H., 11
collectivization, 29
communism, 9
competition, 59-60, 79, 109
Comte, Auguste, 14
cooperatives, 12, 13, 128, 131
corporatism, 46

councils, 17-18, 27-8
Cuba, 5
Czechoslovakia, 42, 94

Darwin, Charles, 14
decentralization, 88, 105, 106, 110, 111,
    117, 133
democracy, 13, 14, 18, 111, 117, 122-5
Devons, Ely, 41, 58
Dickinson, H. D., 53, 58, 59, 82, 84,
    85
Djilas, Milovan, 61
Durbin, E. F. M., 37, 103

Eastern Europe, 42-4, 89
ecology, 3, 26, 110, 133, 134
economic
    calculation, 52-60
    depression, 36, 38
    growth, 4, 5, 42, 44, 48, 67-8, 132
    efficiency, 6, 107-8
élite, 62, 63, 111
Ellman, Michael, 95
employee investment funds, 130
Engels, Friedrich, 7, 9, 71
Erlich, Alexander, 42
European Community (EC), 47, 67

financial institutions, 116, 121, 127
Fourierists, 9
France, 39, 46-7, 114, 115, 126
Frankfurt School, 4

147